"YO! JOEY!"

A BOOK ABOUT SCHOOL LEADERSHIP

JOSEPH P. BATORY

A SCARECROWEDUCATION BOOK

The Scarecrow Press, Inc.
Lanham, Maryland, and London
2002

A SCARECROW EDUCATION BOOK

Published in the United States of America
by Scarecrow Press, Inc.
A Member of the Rowman & Littlefield Publishing Group
4720 Boston Way, Lanham, Maryland 20706
www.scarecrowpress.com

4 Pleydell Gardens, Folkestone
Kent CT20 2DN, England

First Scarecrow Education edition 2002
This Scarecrow Education paperback edition of *"Yo! Joey!" : A Book about School Leadership* is an unabridged republication of the first edition published in Philadelphia in 1999, with the addition of a new subtitle. It is reprinted by arrangement with the author.

British Library Cataloguing in Publication Information Available

Library of Congress Cataloging-in-Publication Data Available

0-8108-4267-X

∞™ The paper used in this publication meets the minimum requirements of American National Standard for Information Sciences—Permanence of Paper for Printed Library Materials, ANSI/NISO Z39.48–1992.
Manufactured in the United States of America.

In memory of my father, Ben, an unpublished author,
and with love, for my wife, Joan

CONTENTS

CONTENTS

CONTENTS

ABOUT THE UPPER DARBY SCHOOL DISTRICT

The Upper Darby School District serves one of the most densely populated municipalities in the Commonwealth of Pennsylvania. Eighty-five thousand people reside within the school system's eight square mile area located on the western edge of Philadelphia.

The community is an inner ring suburb that is transitioning from a homogeneous, white Protestant and Catholic middle class to a much more heterogeneous mix of recent immigrants of multiple origins seeking a better life. There is affordable housing that also attracts many newcomers from Philadelphia. Like many inner ring suburbs, the school district's tax base is declining. Reliance on local property tax increases to support the needs of its burgeoning population is its annual fiscal reality.

The Upper Darby School District's more than eleven thousand students come from diverse social classes and racial groups. The non–English-speaking population is one of the largest in Greater Philadelphia. The Upper Darby School District has responded to its challenges with numerous innovative and progressive initiatives. It has won many awards and honors. All of its schools acknowledge and celebrate ethnic and cultural diversity as a community strength.

The school system offers rich opportunities to its student body. The burden of delivering quality education falls upon the shoulders of the Upper Darby Board of School Directors (nine elected and unpaid officials), and its dedicated administration and teachers, who have excelled at delivering the American Dream at bargain prices.

What you are about to read are the highlights from the experiences and struggles of the educational leader of this community who lived and worked in the middle of this wonderful school system for fifteen years (1984–99). It is the unique autobiographical account of one of America's most outspoken school superintendents.

PROLOGUE

The church was shrouded in darkness. Only the flickering red votive candles in front of each of the three altars offered any illumination. A ten-year-old altar boy, Joey, was the only person inside the church. He had just tolled the outside bell for three minutes to announce to the very Catholic neighborhood that vespers would be held in one hour at 7:30 P.M.

Now that he had done what the hated Sister Ignatius had assigned him to do, Joey was looking for some excitement. He had invited two other altar boy friends, Sal and Rocco, to come over to the unlit church at 6:45 P.M. They would hang out in the darkness together, and shoot the breeze until the parishioners showed up for vespers.

Sal and Rocco would arrive momentarily. Joey had *a gem of an idea*. He grabbed some cassocks from the altar boy wardrobe. This would be a blast!

When his two friends eventually came strolling into the pitch black church through the sacristy entrance, Joey was hiding behind the priest's dressing table. He came up behind them, screamed like a banshee, and threw a cassock over each of their heads. The terrified Sal and Rocco tried to escape, but Joey had them in his grasp. Chaos ensued. The three boys were entangled, fell onto the floor, and then rolled out the doorway onto the main altar.

The three friends stopped wrestling abruptly. Sal and Rocco finally caught on to what had happened. That crazy Joey had pulled another one! The boys sat on the altar steps with cassocks strewn about and laughed hysterically.

Then suddenly, the overhead lights in the church went on. And like your worst dream, the vicious Sister Ignatius was right there glaring at them. She looked like an oversized Hunchback of Notre Dame. And she was mean! The trio froze. They knew they were dead!

The huge nun grabbed the boys by the hair one at a time, dragged them into the sacristy and heaped them into a pile.

Oh God, why have you given me this cross? You have put me in a parish of wild beasts as a test of my faith. Dear Lord, I will not falter. Forgive them, Father. They know not what they have done!

Sister Ignatius then beat the hell out of the three altar boy friends. The nun specialized in rapid-fire slaps, fronthand and backhand to the face. As hard as she tried though, she couldn't make any of the boys cry. The trio took it like men. But, my God, they were only ten years old. The beatings continued.

1

JUST A BIT
ABOUT MY ROOTS

I was born and raised in the street-tough Italian section of Southwest Philadelphia. To an outsider, the old neighborhood could at times appear to be charming. When the dollar-laden Blessed Mother statue was carried through the community at festival time, the place resembled some small town in Tuscany. During daylight hours, you could usually see housewives sweeping and sometimes washing the steps and sidewalks in front of their row houses. And the aroma of spaghetti gravy was ever present.

However, my memories of this densely populated working class community are not that pleasant. Like many other Southwest Philly families, we were poor, and I hated it! As a kid, I managed to find trouble around every corner. I got into more than my share of fights, and lost most of them. The local cops and I were on a first-name basis. I teetered on the edge of disaster through much of my youth. Illusions aside, things were unpredictable and often dangerous in the old neighborhood.

Through my teenage years, I gave absolutely no thought whatsoever to the idea of what I might become some day. Survival was much more of a priority. Career planning? What the hell was that?

When I finished high school, I very nearly followed my father's footsteps into the General Electric factory that employed literally thousands of neighborhood residents and was only six blocks from where we lived. To a young man, it offered immediate money, although no one ever got rich working there. It also yielded a somewhat stable future.

My dad worked in that GE plant for more than thirty-five years. The good news was that he always had a job. The bad news was that he just about made enough money to provide for his wife and five kids. He was really disappointed when I turned down an employment offer to work alongside him and went down a different pathway.

In September of 1960, I did what no one in my immediate family had ever done. I entered college. There was nothing memorable about the experience. I was a stranger in a foreign land. I rode the subways back and forth from our home to northwest Philadelphia's La Salle College every day. I struggled mightily with things academic. I borrowed money and incurred a lot of debt.

The idea of studying to become a doctor or lawyer or accountant or engineer in college never really crossed my mind. I had little or no familiarity with white-collar professions. By default, I eventually ended up as an English-Education major. This wasn't exactly some heavy decision! I hated math and science, and I liked to read. *And I had seen enough rotten teachers in my life.* I figured I could do better than most of the teachers I had if someone would give me a chance.

During my senior year at La Salle, I did the required student teaching at Tilden Junior High School near my home in Southwest Philly. For starters, I had a major problem trying to dress like a teacher because I lacked the appropriate clothing. My next door neighbor was a rock 'n' roll musician and was always buying new clothes. He helped me out by giving me a pretty decent green plaid sportcoat he had planned to discard. However, he was very tall and wore *long* sizes. I needed a *regular,* but this gratis sportcoat was too nice to pass up. The price was sure right! Who cared how well it fit. I did own one pair of black dress pants, but the seat was worn through from excessive use. I put low gloss electricians' tape on the inside of the pants' seat to fix that problem.

And then, my mother had this undertaker friend. Ever wonder what happens to the clothes off a dead body? And so, as I commenced my teaching career, my out-of-style shirt and tie as well as my dress shoes had come off a corpse. My pants were patched, and my green plaid sportcoat was much too large. I really felt sorry for myself, but this student teaching thing had to be done, so I would tough it out.

Just one day into the mission at the close of the school day, a group of African American young ladies from one of my classes came to see me. They fondled my threads and said that I was a "yak," and they all giggled deliciously when they so informed me. I figured they were testing the new teacher. *You have to be tough with these black kids! Can't let them take advantage!*

I dragged the five of them to the principal's office. I reported their crime and demanded that they be disciplined. To my dismay, the principal sent the offenders on their way, and then laughed in my face for two or three minutes. "You damn fool," he declared when he was finally able to talk. "A *yak* is a sharp dresser. Those girls were paying you a compliment on how well you're attired. If anything, you owe them an apology."

Well, I never apologized. I was too humiliated. But I had learned a great lesson about prejudging and stereotyping. I guess everything is relative. So what the hell? Maybe I didn't look so bad after all! I spent the next six months in my student teaching experience trying to make up for my "white boy" stupidity. I found out that I could teach! And that I liked it.

I actually was graduated from La Salle on schedule in June of 1964 with a 2.6 academic index (out of a possible 4.0). For me, this was no small feat. I applied to teach in many suburban Philadelphia school districts. No one wanted any part of me. I did get close to one job in an affluent school district in Delaware County (PA). They had an opening for a secondary English teacher. I had a great interview with the school's principal. He sent me to meet the superintendent of schools. He was one of those obsessed with the Mayflower elitists who prioritize unilateral ownership of the United States. His primary concern was with my ethnic heritage. As soon as he asked the question, I knew I had no chance for the job. And, of course, I didn't get it.

In September of 1964, two days before school was scheduled to open, a miracle happened. I landed my first real job, a teaching position with the only school district in the world that would touch me . . . the Camden, New Jersey Public Schools.

2

THE TRAINING GROUND

And so I began my illustrious career as an educator, facing the formidable challenges of being a teacher in Camden, New Jersey. Funny thing was that I really loved the Camden experience. A marvelous training ground for someone serious about education. At twenty-one years of age, I was very serious. I also needed work. It was great to get hired anywhere, even Camden!

Mostly, I taught English and Reading to seventh and eighth graders. Budding teenagers full of unrestrained energy. Couple that with them being city kids and the task for any teacher would be formidable to say the least. I was up for the challenge.

My philosophy of teaching was about to evolve. Lots of people had told me to start out tough, and it would pay off in classroom dividends later on. I wasn't exactly sure whether or not to follow that strategy. But after experiencing my first work day in the Camden Public Schools, I was absolutely convinced that this was infallible advice.

I had headed off a potential fight among seven or eight female thugs glaring at one another menacingly before school even got underway that morning. As I dispersed the would-be combatants, I got plenty of hard stares. New teacher, huh? Thinks he's some big shot! We'll get him later!

Then, as I had my initial meeting with a group of eighth graders behaving too good to be true in homeroom (first appearances are always deceiving), there was a commotion in the hallway. An elderly female teacher was chasing a pack of ruffians who had obviously just pulled her wig off her head. The mob was running down the corridor with their prize in hand, and the distraught woman in hot pursuit.

I stepped outside my classroom doorway, put out my right leg, and tripped the lead gangster. You had to think fast in Camden. The perp skidded one way. And the wig went flying in another direction. I confiscated the wig and screamed at the thieves to line up against the wall. The kids ignored me, and scattered into the building catacombs. I handed the humiliated woman her hair. She was most grateful and quite devastated.

Welcome to teaching in Camden. This was a no-brainer. Only the strong would survive in this place. I immediately assumed the demeanor of Attila the Hun and went back into my homeroom to strike fear into the hearts of my pupils.

From that threshold moment onward, I orchestrated every opening of school with the same dictatorial authority. It worked well. Students were awestruck if not just plain scared. *Who was this madman?* I was the strictest, most demanding teacher any of them had ever seen. I called lots of bluffs and backed down the toughest kids. I never smiled. I piled on work. The reign of terror usually lasted for six to eight weeks.

Ah, the wonders of hypnotic therapy. Gradually, after about two months of boot camp, the feared Gestapo man would now disappear. Because by psychological magic, I now owned my students' minds and souls. They would stay firmly in my grasp no matter what. I still kept the academic faucets turned on. But now I transformed myself into some kinder and gentler teacher my pupils had never before met. For the many remaining months of each school year, non-stop zaniness and the outrageously funny were my trademarks. I was one wild and crazy guy!

English class became daily fun. I told a few thousand humorous anecdotes. I dressed in costumes and disguises. I walked on student desks. I role-played, satirized, and hyperbolized about everything and anything, usually with props. Often my students and I would laugh so hard that we cried. But the amazing thing was that I could get complete order and control in an instant any time I wanted it.

I gave my Camden kids writing assignments three times a week. Insanity for an English teacher. Too much paper work for one human to handle. But I was young and filled with the idealistic dream that I would make a difference. I read each and every piece of student writing and showered my authors with glowing feedback and encouraging, flattering comments no matter what the actual quality of their products. *Get them to write. Worry about the quality later.* It involved a ton of work and was absolutely worth it.

Kids soon *wanted* to write for me. So I buried them with writing assignments. Incredibly enough, they thought all this work was neat. When all was said and done, I had twelve- and thirteen-year-olds originating a hundred or so pieces of writing each during the school year. They had to get better doing this. And they did. Of course, they also had my brilliant "how to" instruction, and my relentless positive reinforcement. Exhausting and exhilarating for yours truly. The best days of my life. Teaching in, of all places, Camden, New Jersey.

I've always equated teaching with saving people. In Camden, teachers were lifeguards. Humans drowning everywhere. I saved plenty of kids when I worked there. Jonathan Kozol has a striking chapter about life in Camden in *Savage Inequalities: Children in America's Schools*. I always say that he captured it. But I lived in it—and more than survived it.

In later years as a superintendent of schools, I consistently lectured to faculties and principals that mediocre teachers all too often take kids as they come to them, label them, quantify them, and endorse these youngsters' background and baggage with low grades. However, great teachers, I stressed, effect some positive change in *every* kid, no matter what level of ability or what problems they bring in with them from the outside world. Great teachers never look at young people for what they are, but rather for what they might become. *Great teachers make the difference for all kids, and especially the ones everybody else has written off.* My passionate philosophy of education in Camden—and to this day.

3

DON'T MESS WITH
THE PRINCIPAL!

Federal money abounded for education in the middle 1960s. Lyndon Johnson's Great Society initiatives were everywhere. One of the most successful programs was Operation Headstart, an attempt to bridge gaps between privileged and underprivileged children. For two summers, I made extra money teaching four-and-a-half-year-olds during July and August. It was a surprisingly good experience. Fertile minds. Energy without limits. You could make a difference here.

I must have been doing something right because only three years into my career as an educator, I was made a summertime Headstart principal. For several years, in July and August, I headed up a school which had seven hundred of the poorest children you could ever imagine. To some this would be intimidating. To me it was terrifying. I was a twenty-four-year-old white boy in charge of a ghetto school full of minority children with awesome needs.

I don't want to bore you with too many stories of my survival in the inner city. But to learn about my management style, Camden is a good place to start. The Cooper's Poynt School was a newer facility amidst the deprivation of North Camden. It was where I presided over my Headstart Lilliputians. Catty-corner to the school was one of the scummy bars for which Camden was famous. A small army of winos and vagrants sat outside the bar on the steps twenty-four hours each day, begging nickels and free drinks from the regulars. Since the bartender owners had baseball bats and guns to fend off nonpaying customers, these ragtags were restricted to the steps outside the bar 99 percent of the time. And when the bums needed to relieve themselves, what better idea than to cross the street and use the lavatories inside Cooper's Poynt School. Right alongside my Headstart kids.

Early on, I decided to put an end to this nonsense. Don't mess with me. I'm the principal! I rounded up my parent council and teacher leaders and we developed a solution together. Done just like they tell you to do it in graduate schools of education. A consensus solution arrived at democratically.

New locks were put on the lavatories. Teachers had the keys. We had complete control.

If only things were that simple. So the lavatories were locked. Big deal! Within days, the derelicts were substituting school lobbies and closets as their urinals and toilets.

Now, I was really ticked off. This time I meant business. I trekked to the local police station and demanded action. The next day, I got it. The Camden cops showed up in force and chased all the loiterers and promised more of the same every day. This might have worked. Except that one of these law enforcement geniuses had to go and tell the ejectees that this was all the brilliant idea of that meddling principal across the street.

Two days later, after the kids and most of the teachers had gone home for the afternoon, and when the school was occupied solely by my secretary, Leola, and yours truly, we had a visitor. He was in the reception area just outside my office colorfully explaining to Leola that he was in our office on a specific mission to cut off the testicles of this principal who couldn't mind his own business. I heard Leola's fearful sobs. And I thought seriously about exiting through my office window, but I didn't.

Once again, you can sense my lack of practical wisdom. Somehow, I screwed up my courage. I went out to meet my adversary. The killer was well over six feet tall and held a twelve-inch blade in his right hand. His eyes were glazed over. No one home in there. Well, when a nasty dog barks, bark back!

I burst out of my office and shouted at the villain in my deepest voice: "You want the (deleted expletive) principal. Well I'm telling you the (deleted expletive) principal's not here. He's gone for the summer and won't be back for four more weeks. So you're just wasting your (deleted expletive) time and ours!" After all, I was only the summertime principal. No sense in him killing a small fry part-timer. The wino was taken aback. Leola's eyes nearly burst out of her head. She had never heard me use the vernacular.

"Look, you want to do a number on the principal, that's fine with me," I bravely continued in my best calming tone. "He's not back from vacation yet. If you want, I'll write down the date he'll be back. But right now, my secretary and I are goin' home!"

The mad dog was confused. Damn good thing. He lowered the knife. He pondered his dilemma. Looked like he might be willing to wait for a bigger fish. "I's sorry about this," our uninvited guest politely muttered. "I'll try to come back when he's in. Didn't mean to keep you from goin' home." I exhaled with a deep sense of relief. Score another point for strategic problem-solving ability.

Leola, the wino, and I walked out of the school together like good buddies. And I never saw the killer again. Leadership tactics from the school of streets. And no, I have no idea whether or not some former Camden principal is walking around these days with a scar on his face. Get real here! Leola and I were about to become new residents of the city morgue. Good school administrators do what they have to do in this world!

4

IF YOU NEED
SOMETHING DONE,
ACT LIKE A MANIAC!

One final tidbit from my Camden experiences would probably add to your understanding of my managerial prowess. While I was doing my principal thing at the Headstart Center during the summer of 1968, the school telephones began to malfunction. The phones would go totally dead for two to three hours, come back on, then go dead again and so forth. Not exactly a good situation when you have seven hundred preschoolers under your care in the building. For several days, in response to our pleas for help, a few apathetic telephone workers came and went. Each time, they promised me the problem was fixed. And each time, it wasn't.

One morning after the phones went down again, my fuse blew. I drove to a nearby school and called the phone company headquarters. I heaped a torrent of abuse and threats on three secretaries until I got to the top. I was able to arrange for the area vice president to come on site that afternoon to view the difficulty firsthand. I had to work fast.

I drove back to my phoneless Headstart Center and removed all the furniture from my office except my swivel chair and of course my desk. Next, I grabbed a mini-chair used to seat little children from one of my classrooms and placed it in the center of my office. I was ready for my "big bopper" visitor.

If you need something to happen and it's not happening in the workplace, act like a maniac. Guaranteed success! Leola showed the executive visitor, clad in his three-piece suit, into my suddenly sparse office. She took one look at the kindergarten-size chair in the center of the room and ran for cover.

CHAPTER 4

The vice president offered his hand. I ignored it. Then he tried, "Good afternoon." "You must be some kind of nut," I shouted at him. "You're in a school for little children with no phones working. How in the hell could this be a good afternoon? Sit down. I'm going to talk. And you're going to listen!"

The bewildered executive hesitated only for an instant. Surely I was deranged, he must have thought. He must have been concerned that I could also be dangerous, so he sat down in the child's chair, the only available piece of furniture to him. He looked ridiculous. It almost made up for the aggravation his company had caused my school. But not quite.

From behind the desk, I looked down on him like he was a bad kid. I gave him lots of bluster and bluff. I said that I had contacted the NAACP regarding this unforgivable treatment of minority children. I told my visitor that I would be calling all of the Greater Philadelphia television stations about this travesty immediately upon his departure. And I further indicated that he could expect several hundred parent pickets at his company's headquarters in the morning. As the coup de grace, I threw some books at the wall, and yelled at this dimwit to "get the hell out of my office." The corporate fool went out in a hurry. Whew! Acting was hard work.

Within an hour, armies of telephone workers were on the scene. Within two hours, all the telephones were working. And we never had the problem again.

5

THE NEW
SUPERINTENDENT
GETS A VISIT FROM
HIS PAST

Forget whatever romantic crap you've ever read or heard about setting goals as the key to success. It's not relevant. At least, not in my case.

I left teaching and the Camden Public Schools in 1970. By this time, I had earned a master's degree. I was able to become an administrator at my alma mater, La Salle College, where I worked for the next five years. I didn't think that anybody could have paid worse than a public school system. I forgot about Catholic colleges. There was no future for me at La Salle. I had to get out.

In 1975, I crossed back into public education. I entered the Upper Darby School District at the very bottom of the Central Administration pile. I certainly had no illusions or plans regarding advancement. It was just a better-paying entry-level job. What did happen, however, were several accidents of fate, a few timely twists and turns of life, and some fortunate occasions where I was in the right place at the right time. I went from the very bottom to the very top. It took nine years.

October 1, 1984, was my first day as the Upper Darby School District's superintendent of schools. On that date, I became the CEO of the largest and most diverse school system in Delaware County, Pennsylvania, located just west of Philadelphia. On the way to work, I had driven past about twenty of my nearly one hundred bright yellow school busses scurrying about the community to pick up kids. It occurred to me that these were *my* busses serving *my* schools. I was now the ruler of my empire of eight thousand students and eight hundred employees. It felt great. I'd come a long way from the streets of Southwest Philly.

To begin my first day as boss, I spent about an hour pondering the executive mahogany furniture that came with the superintendent's office. I'm a philosophical thinker by nature. I thought about the history of the Upper Darby School District. Only five previous superintendents in the twentieth century. I was number six and, at forty years old, the youngest to ever get to the top. Some school districts throw out a superintendent every year. But Upper Darby had tradition. Leaders here lasted. A great confidence builder for a starting superintendent. I put my feet up on the huge glass top desk and smelled the power. If the guys from my old school yard could see me now. This was heavy stuff.

Anne was my administrative assistant. She was an attractive woman a few years older than me. Anne had wisdom, common sense, and people skills in abundance. I had worked in the school system for ten years. Lots of nice people there, but not so many you could trust. Anne you could trust. We became mutual problem solvers while she worked for the last superintendent and I was the assistant superintendent. Anne also had class. She was my reminder that I was no longer in Southwest Philly. When she came into my office that morning, I quickly pulled my feet off the desk.

"You have your first call, Mr. 'First Day' Superintendent," Anne twinkled with curiosity. "It's someone named Guido. He says you'll know who he is." It was like *a spear in the heart*. I knew this would happen! My past was haunting me already. The only Guido that I knew was the neighborhood bookie from twenty-five years ago. Then, as a teenager, I had envied him. Now, here in my glorious present, I didn't want any part of him. This couldn't be happening. My God, Guido!

"Anne, I think that that's a personal call so I'd rather not take it right now," I cleverly stated. When in doubt, a school superintendent evades! "Tell him I'm in conference and that I'll get back to him if he'll leave a number." An imperial administrative command. *Get rid of him!* I could always think fast when I sensed trouble. Anne shrugged and left to handle Guido. I put my feet back up on the desk. My best thinking position, and I needed to think. Guido! God help me!

I had heard something about Guido just about a year before the phone call. An old high school friend of mine had seen Guido in front of a judge in a Philadelphia courtroom. I had assumed he was in jail. For all I knew, he was calling from prison. Well, why not? I had plenty of employees in the school system. He probably wanted to use my school district as a base for a small gambling operation. No way I was going to talk with this shadow from my past.

The best thing about Anne was that she knew when to leave something alone. After I again told her to get rid of Guido after his third telephone call that day, she stopped bothering me about Guido. I couldn't say how many similar calls came in the next two days.

Perhaps the Guido episode would have just gone away. Matter of fact, I'm sure that it would have just vaporized had I not decided to share the incident with my confessor, my first and lasting true love, and my one and only wife, Joan. She never knew Guido, but that wouldn't have mattered. She had decided what I should do.

"You can't deny your roots or run from your past," the beautiful Joan suggested as we shared some very dry martinis at home two nights after Guido's first call. "Get on the phone tomorrow and talk to him! He's where you came from, and you owe him at least a return call." Easy for her to say. She wouldn't have to talk to him. I would. But I obeyed as usual. Prime requisite for a long standing marriage. *Wife commands and husband complies.* So the next morning, I called Guido.

"Guido, my main man. Sorry I took so long to get back to you. What a great surprise to hear from you. Whaddya need?" I braced for the worst. The cops were probably going to be wire-tapping Guido's illegal requests. They would hear it all. I would be indicted with him.

"Joey, I'm just so unbelievably proud of you," Guido bubbled. I waited for the punch line. "Someone from our neighborhood getting up there in the world so far. I just wanted to wish you the very best. You've really made it, kid, like I always said you would. Cent' anni!"

Okay, so I'm wrong once in a while. Contrary to my paranoiac beliefs, there were no requests from Guido that we engage in criminal activity together. Instead, Guido and I waxed nostalgically about people, places, and things from the old neighborhood. I had ashamedly forgotten about Guido's influence in my life. He was only three or four years older than me. Back then, he had acted like the big brother I never had. Guido was always lecturing me. He must have viewed me as a Southwest Philly angel with a dirty face. He had decided to save me!

I would have killed to become one of his runners. His workers had nice cars, pretty girls, and money. But Guido had another vision for me. He refused to hire me despite my numerous requests. And I remember that Guido was the first person in my life to tell me that I could compete successfully with those from higher birth. He was always badgering me to work at it, academically and legally.

I guess you could say that at least in part I'm the protégé of a bookie. And how many superintendents of schools can say that? Guido was choked up and sobbing through much of our conversation. I deserved to feel stupid and small and I did! Score another point for my wife, Joan, the advisor—right on as usual.

"Three things before I sign off," said Guido. "First, I won't bother you again. You're busy enough. Second, just concentrate on the kids who are like you were. Them's the ones that need the help. And third, if anybody gets in the way of what you want to do, just let me know and they'll be taken care of. Thanks for talkin' to me, Joey. Don't waste this golden opportunity. It's your chance of a lifetime."

When I got off the phone, I was flooded with emotion. One of my prime traits. My past had come back for a short visit and it wasn't so bad at all. Anne wandered into the office with some papers to sign. I quickly pulled my feet off the glass top desk. She took one look into my tear-filled eyes and abruptly left. She really did know when to leave something alone!

6

NOW THAT
I'M FAMOUS

After recovering from the reappearance of Guido in my life, I was raven-
ously hungry. Joan and I had just purchased a house in the school district, and I usually ate lunch at our home only minutes away from the office.
However, today I headed for the local diner. The neighborhood hash house
was bustling with blue collar workers on lunch breaks and senior citizen regulars. My kind of place. Tough waitresses, strong coffee, cigarette smoke
everywhere, and plates banging away. Noisy and colorful. Big portions.

I ordered scrapple and eggs and greasy home fries, a traditional Philly
breakfast that I really loved. The food arrived quickly, and I was in gastro-
nomic heaven. Eventually, I noticed an elderly couple two tables away sneak-
ing repeated glances at me. It was obvious I had been recognized. I read the
woman's lips. "That's him," she kept telling her husband. "That's him!"
Celebrity status already. I had indeed arrived. I basked in the glow!

As I was exiting the diner, the admiring female senior citizen grabbed me
by the arm. "I know who you are. My husband and I would know you anywhere. We just love the job you're doing for Upper Darby!" she exclaimed.
"This is such an honor. Can I have your autograph?"

She handed me a plain white envelope for the signature. I was really flat-
tered. I smiled my best smile. "The honor will be all mine. But I'd like to per-
sonalize it for you," I suggested with the appropriate humility. "What's your
first name?"

"Oh, Congressman Edgar, you are so kind," she replied. "Just address it
to Melanie. I can't wait to show this to all my friends."

CHAPTER 6

The red alert buzzer exploded in my brain. This misguided soul thought I was Bob Edgar, the Seventh District U.S. Representative, a Democrat who kept confounding the local Republican party by winning elections in an area in which they held a huge majority. Well, so be it. I signed her envelope: *Best wishes to my dearest friend, Melanie!!!!! Congressman Bob Edgar.* I went back to work. So much for being famous.

7

THE LADY IN RED

The very next day, I drove to Harrisburg. My predecessor, Mike, who had taught me many things about administration while I was his assistant, had explained that the key to the enigmatic Pennsylvania Department of Education (PDE) was in knowing the right person. He advised me to ignore all of the high-level bureaucrats with their fancy titles. Most of them in his view would just waste my time. Just find out who the person is that really makes things happen. Forget the rest.

With nearly a thousand employees, our school district always had many questions about the mysteries of teacher and administrator certification. Right before he retired, Mike told me that Diana was the right person in certification. No nonsense. Gets to the heart of the matter. Finds you the answer pronto. At Mike's suggestion, I was heading to Harrisburg to establish my relationship with Diana over lunch.

I think I had been to the PDE offices only once in my life. A thousand sterile cubicles in a cold concrete building. A bunch of faceless, dazed blockheads wandering around. I roamed through the maze and finally got escorted into Diana's small office. I didn't know quite what to expect.

Diana was extremely attractive with long blond hair combed straight down to the small of her back. She had on a shiny red top of some sort. But, believe it or not, I wasn't even looking at her. Instead, I was magnetized by the walls which were filled with Clint Eastwood photographs from his movies. Most curious, indeed!

CHAPTER 7

Diana rose up to greet me, and I saw that her red top was part of an *extremely short* leather mini-skirt suit. Now she had my attention. Diana had on shiny, high-heeled matching red boots over a pair of shapely legs. Forget about Clint Eastwood! I was gaping at Diana. And I couldn't take my eyes off her. Diana had piercing green eyes that had probably melted many a man. I was no exception; I was already melted! We exchanged pleasantries, and she excused herself for just a minute. I took some deep breaths. I rechecked all the Clint Eastwood pictures. It helped my blood pressure go down.

However, it got worse when Diana returned. Because I now got the full view of her voluptuous body bursting out from beneath her tight leather clothes as she wiggled toward me. Someone turn on the air conditioning; I'm burning up! Diana was ready for lunch. Eat? Who wanted to eat?

She had decided it was such a beautiful day that we should walk about five blocks to a French restaurant she loved. It suddenly occurred to me that maybe as a new school superintendent, I didn't want to be seen wandering through the streets of Harrisburg on a school day with this stunning and very sexy woman. *Beware the appearance of evil.* That's what I always told my junior high students. Thank heavens I had my sunglasses with me. I put them on immediately while still inside the PDE building.

Diana and I strolled through Harrisburg's streets. She turned every male head. We finally got to the intimate, dark restaurant. Wow. A gorgeous woman and she was all mine. By this time, I was having all kinds of interesting fantasies. They ended quickly.

I may have been smitten, but Diana was all business. She focused the discussion, answered my many questions, and made considerable sense for me out of the confusion of the Department of Education. We enjoyed a wonderful, expensive lunch that I paid for. Worth every dollar!

I walked her back to her office, and then promptly returned to Upper Darby. We had established a solid working relationship that lasted for many years. Diana answered a thousand certification inquiries and solved a myriad of problems for my teachers and administrators during my fifteen years as superintendent. And maybe it all could have been so much more. If only I looked more like Clint Eastwood!

8

A LITTLE HELP
FROM MY FRIENDS

Shortly thereafter, I presided over a difficult school board meeting as superintendent. It was stormy. The regular "complainers and moaners" were all there. People with no lives who substitute the public forum for joy in life. Vitriolic public statements abounded. The school board was accused of so many crimes you would think they were pornographers and child molesters instead of unpaid public servants overseeing the public schools. It was all very ugly. The school board members were remarkably restrained. Our board had an unwritten rule about avoiding meaningless confrontations. It was regularly reiterated to us all by Teresa, the legendary board president we all loved.

And then the critics started on me. What was I going to do about a host of things these experts wanted done? What do you people think? That I've got some magic wand? I've only been on the job a few days! Some of the speakers took personal shots. I nearly bit my tongue off keeping my mouth shut. I held my temper in check. Well, thank you so much for the kind words to your superintendent! Meanwhile the four news reporters wrote feverishly.

The meeting finally ended and I went home in a sweat-soaked suit. Joan was asleep, so I ate peanut butter, drank lots of beer, and felt sorry for myself. I didn't get much sleep. The only good thing I could think of was that there wouldn't be another public meeting until next month. For my money, that was far too soon.

When November's board meeting eventually rolled around, I was despondent and apprehensive. I was supposed to be an important leader of the community. Instead, I was about to again be nailed to a cross for my monthly crucifixion. I was really stressed out!

Then, ten minutes before the session was scheduled to start, I had a strange vision. Pacing back and forth in the back of the boardroom was Rocco, an acquaintance from the old neighborhood whom I hadn't see in a very long time. Rocco was also the toughest Italian stallion you ever wanted to avoid. I figured I had gone over the cliff and that I was seeing things, but I decided to confront the apparition. I headed for the back of the room.

"Rocco, paisan, is that you? It must be twenty years. What are you doing here at a school board meeting?" Not very profound, but I didn't exactly know what else to say. Rocco's muscular upper body nearly popped the seams and buttons off his white silk shirt. His shiny black hair was combed back and tied into a pony tail. He was definitely here for business.

"Joey, you just get up there and do whatever you do at these meetings. I'll take care of any problem people!" Spoken as Rocco always did. Few words but on point. "Anybody starts on you tonight, I'm gonna break their legs."

Say what? Talk about getting my attention. I nearly had a stroke. A real life murder novel in the making! *Death in the Boardroom.* School superintendent as an accomplice to the killer. My career in shambles.

"Rocco, don't do this," I begged. "This is America. People are allowed to be critical of anything, including me."

"Joey, just do the meeting, and I'll take care of business back here," Rocco said with his best glazed look. "It's been decided. Any repeat of last month's dumping on you by anyone is a death wish!"

At certain times rational persuasion is useless. This was one of them. Rocco was on a mission. The board president gaveled the meeting to order. And I wondered who among the public gathering was about to die.

My career as a superintendent could easily have ended that evening. Rocco was ready to wreak havoc! But for whatever reason, the public speakers at that meeting were few, well-reasoned, and polite. Last month's antagonists were "no shows." Must have been something special on television. All was peace and tranquillity.

Rocco looked disappointed. After the meeting, I hugged him with a great sense of relief and thanked him for his "help." But Rocco said he would probably be back next month just to be sure things continued like tonight.

Nobody was gonna mess up my career as a school superintendent. That was the word. I was a protected species.

Salvatore had one of those classic Roman noses. He was the boss of what law enforcement calls a criminal organization. He and I grew up on the same street in Southwest Philly. Early on, we were the best of friends. As teenagers, we drifted apart. In the late 1950s, he headed up a teenage gang. His internship, I suppose. Sal moved in the fast lane. By the time we were both sixteen years old, Sal was already a high school dropout. I was bogged down with the peculiar artificiality of the academic track in high school. Our paths rarely crossed.

But then one night as I was walking back from my second home, the only lighted community basketball court, some ten blocks from my house, I found Sal moaning and bleeding in an alley. He was badly beaten and begged me to get him out of there before "they came back for him." My idea was to get the cops or run back to the neighborhood to get help.

However, my opinions didn't count for too much with a wounded gang leader. Sal directed; I followed. I got him up on his feet, supported his sagging bulk on my shoulders, and we staggered the many blocks back to the street where we lived. Sal's father and mother and brothers were strangely silent when they saw him. Obviously they were used to this kind of stuff. My family would have been hysterical.

I said I had to get home and I left. But not before Sal's dad grabbed me around the back of my neck and kissed me on both cheeks in front of the family. He told me my heroic conduct would never be forgotten. In the days that followed, neighborhood buzz had it that I had carried a wounded Sal back from some war through enemy fire and a mine field. I liked the legend immensely. And lots of people believed it!

Now, twenty-five years later and two days after my most recent school board meeting, I sat in the back of Our Lady of Loreto Church in Southwest Philadelphia alongside Sal in a pew. He was immaculately groomed in a $500 suit and reeked of expensive cologne. I was clad in one of my Sear's "two for $150" suits, which was wrinkled from my having worked all day. We had a 4:00 P.M. appointment.

"Joey, I can't understand you. I'm trying to help you. You deserve respect as a school superintendent. Why should you have to listen to a bunch of hot air from ignorant sheep? They need to be taught to be respectful," summarized Sal after about fifteen minutes of our conversation. "You're an educator. Look at this as necessary lessons for them that needs it."

"Sal, please. It's not that I'm not really grateful. But if you do this, then I'll never truly know whether or not I can cut it as a superintendent," I pleaded for about the twentieth time. "I've got to try this on my own. I understand what you're saying, but to give me a fair shot, you've got to back off."

A silence ensued. Sal was mulling all of this over. I watched his well-dressed bodyguards at each church entrance. Finally, Sal spoke: "Joey, I'll do what you want. We'll just leave things alone for awhile. But you're makin' a mistake. I know how you are. You'll try to save the world in them schools. And you'll probably get yourself into a pack of trouble. You're wasting assistance that lots of others beg for and don't get. Okay, you do this your way. You always were a stubborn knucklehead! We wuz just tryin' to get you off on the right foot."

I thanked Sal profusely and said goodbye. He wrapped his huge hands around my neck like his father had once done and kissed me on both cheeks. Sal then went up to the altar to light some votive candles. Probably figured he better start praying for me. As I left Our Lady of Loreto Church, I felt more unsure, more insecure, and more lonely than ever before in my life. I had to be crazy. I had just turned down a wonderful security blanket. Who me, practical? The last rugged individual, that's what I was. Sounded like a recipe for disaster.

9

A TOUCH OF THE IVY

I completed all the graduate work necessary to get my certification as a school superintendent at the University of Pennsylvania. When I first matriculated there, I was filled with excitement. Free thinking and open minds at an Ivy institution!

I carried two courses simultaneously to begin my studies in educational administration at Penn. One of them was some sort of sociology offering where we were required to read Lillian Breslow Rubin's *Worlds of Pain*. I started perusing the assigned work on a Sunday afternoon while watching the Philadelphia Eagles against the New York Giants on television. I couldn't put the book down. Matter of fact, I actually shut off the TV. The hell with the stupid Eagles! I was fascinated by this remarkable portrait of working-class people based on the writer's firsthand observation. It was all very reminiscent of what I saw all around me while growing up in Southwest Philly. It was something I could really relate to. I devoured the book. I couldn't wait to go to my next class at Penn.

Sure enough, when our class reconvened, we were put in a seminar circle facing one another. Boy, was I ready. The professor asked for input. I jumped right in. I gave *Worlds of Pain* rave reviews. Two thumbs up! I commented on its realism and accurate depiction of working class people. And then my whole world collapsed.

Most of my graduate colleagues panned the book. Some of my classmates were of the opinion that a world like Rubin had described couldn't possibly exist. A few said it was an exaggerated version of the working class.

CHAPTER 9

Still others actually accused the author of making up the content of her many interviews. It was all some sophomoric game of "oneupsmanship" that these Penn graduate students were playing. Stupid me! I wanted to talk about the issue of the working class in American society.

I was boiling. I got a wee bit loud and somewhat emotional. The professor suggested that I was perhaps too subjective about this topic. My classmates nodded solemnly. But I was 100 percent sure that this book was on the money! If I didn't know about the working class, who did?

Through the many remaining weeks of this course, I kept trying to add my viewpoints on whatever we were addressing. No one was listening. I was like John the Baptist, the voice of a loose cannon crying out in the wilderness. I really began wondering what I was doing at the University of Pennsylvania.

In my other graduate class, I ran into an avowed Marxist professor. He was a true believer, pontificating all the theoretical wonders of communism while the only real examples in the world that I was aware of were despicable totalitarian states. He also spent a great deal of time condemning schooling in capitalist America, although I'm fairly certain that he never set foot in a public school in any professional capacity. How the hell could he be an expert on schooling in America? Well, I guess he was just another omniscient professor. In the spirit of academia, I decided to take him on.

The professor was really filled up with himself. The graduate class of about twenty students, mostly young women, swooned over his every word. Those British accents work every time. I waited for some debate. It never came, so I created it.

All I really did was to bring into question some of the shortcomings of Marxism in actual practice. I also challenged the professor's biased views of public schools. The guy was generalizing about what went on in more than 80,000 American public schools. I told him so in front of the class. So maybe it's not such a good idea to debate with the course instructor!

I should have seen the writing on the wall when my classmates glared at me in horror whenever I opened my mouth. Hell, it was one of my first courses at Penn. How was I supposed to know how to behave? I'm from Southwest Philly!

The professor launched vitriolic rebuttals against whatever I said whenever I said it, although he never made eye contact. He regularly referred to me as "a silly defender of the status quo" while gazing intently at the ceiling of the classroom. What the hell was he looking at up there? I wanted to punch his lights out.

Of course, the professor got lots of support from his adoring fans. I got none. Was I in the People's Republic of Karl Marx or at the University of Pennsylvania? I thought differences of opinion were allowed here. Where in blazes were my academic freedom and my rights as a student? I was ready to quit, but I didn't.

After this shaky start, things at Penn improved dramatically for me. In the next four years, I experienced many enlightening courses and some wonderful professors. I read prolifically in the field. I actually enjoyed the university experience. And I became a straight A student.

10

TESTING, TESTING . . . 1, 2, 3

In the mid-1980s, the Pennsylvania Department of Education (PDE) began administering standardized tests statewide. The results of these tests were supposed to reveal which schools were getting the job done and which ones weren't. An idiotic and unfounded conclusion if ever there was one.

When the test data were eventually made public, the results largely validated the social-class status of school districts. School systems with advantaged populations of affluent white kids had vastly higher test scores than the working class and poor schools as well as systems that were primarily composed of racial and ethnic minorities. You didn't have to be a genius to have predicted these outcomes.

Did we really need to spend millions of dollars for this testing? Maybe it had political value for Harrisburg's bureaucrats, but educationally it was incredibly stupid. One superintendent of schools from one of the most wealthy communities in Pennsylvania rejoiced in his school district's great test scores so he called a press conference to proclaim his district "number one." Nothing like bragging about a self-fulfilling prophecy. Advantaged kids showing off their advantage.

On the other side of the fence, urban school districts bottomed out on the test. Let's hear it for the brilliant ones from PDE! They ignored the backgrounds of the kids. They promoted racial and social-class stereotyping. And they communicated to the most needy students and their teachers and families and school that they weren't worth much. Those were the real results of this state testing debacle.

Closer to home in my own Upper Darby School District, our tests scores were mediocre. And why not? With tremendous socioeconomic diversity, student mobility, increasing numbers of immigrant pupils whose first language wasn't English, and many other refugees from Philadelphia's schools, what exactly would a generalized quantified test composite tell anyone? That we had lots of kids with needs. No kidding!

Just like at Penn, I waited for some debate. There wasn't any once again. The news media gave credibility to this state testing program and sensationalized the results across Pennsylvania. The educational establishment was quite silent. How could this be happening?

I authored my first ever opinion article. I sent it to *The Philadelphia Inquirer*. When the paper notified me that they were going to publish it, I was distraught. Why do I do these things? What was a relatively new school superintendent doing out there on the point? Where were all the veteran educational leaders with brains?

The screaming banner head in the morning *Inquirer* of October 8, 1988, read "Beam me up, Scotty. There's no intelligent life down here." My byline was prominently positioned right under the headline. In the article, I blasted the Pennsylvania Department of Education for its ridiculous misuse of testing. I decried this portrayal of standardized test results as some ultimate measure of students. So many of my kids needed time to develop and blossom academically, and in time, they would. I wondered in the article if any of Harrisburg's bureaucrats had ever done any graduate work or read any books about variables that influence research. And I chastised colleague school administrators who used this test data for their own self-adulation. What a way to win friends!

It was late afternoon the same day when Anne walked into my office and said she had the Pennsylvania Department of Education on the telephone. This could be trouble. I had her put the call through.

"The Secretary is very upset!" said the bureaucrat in his firmest and most important voice. The reference to the secretary of course meant Pennsylvania's Secretary of Education. I guess this was supposed to scare me. Now, let's get something straight here. Sal and Rocco I'm afraid of! Some Secretary of Education hardly worried me. The caller continued: "We in Harrisburg don't think kindly of your article in *The Philadelphia Inquirer* this morning. Your lack of recognition of the importance of testing is disturbing to us. I would remind you that we have commissioned you as an officer of the state. Revocation of your license is not out of the question."

I never liked being threatened. I was seething. "Tell the Secretary that he's not nearly as upset as I am," I exploded. "Tell the Secretary that misusing test results only hurts what caring educators are trying to do. Tell the Secretary that getting out of his office and into some schools to see what's really going on is a much better idea than wasting taxpayer dollars on this testing boondoggle. And tell the Secretary not to use some flunky to communicate his messages." I hung up. And I hadn't even used one bad word! I was so proud of myself.

I didn't hear any more from Harrisburg and settled back in to my daily routines. Two days later, on returning to work after lunch, I came upon a well-dressed young man talking to Anne in the outer office. He had identified himself as a state auditor and was requesting an inspection of professional credentials—mine! I then interrupted and told our guest that I was the one to see about this. I invited him into my office. He wasn't quite sure who or what I was.

"These are my credentials. I'm sure you'll find them satisfactory." I said, pointing to pictures of students that covered an entire wall. "That's me in all of them. I'm mostly teaching or visiting classes, but there's a few with me giving awards. Those are my credentials. What else do you need?" The auditor began to sense that he was in the presence of someone without a full deck.

The visitor was very nervous. He pleaded his case: "Look, I don't enjoy doing this. But I was told to verify your certification and your commission and inspect your personnel file. The pictures are nice, but not what I'm after."

"Oh, I know what you're after," I sarcastically responded. "You've been sent to find witches and goblins and other devils. Fortunately for you, today is your lucky day. Because you're going to walk out of here in one piece. Besides you're probably just following orders, so I am not going to be my usual nasty self.

"Anne will give you whatever you want, but I just wanted you to learn firsthand the difference between a school system and the bureaucrats you work for. Here in this school district we deal with the growth and development of those young people in the pictures. You and your Harrisburg friends deal with meaningless crap. I'd appreciate it very much if you'd convey my little message to your superiors. Now, get the hell out of my office, and do what you have to do."

Relieved to be out of my unstable clutches, the auditor scrambled out of my office. Anne had my personnel file ready for him. He spent only about two minutes perusing it. I can't imagine what his vindictive bosses thought they were going to find. And if they were just trying to harass me, I don't think it worked. The state auditor expediently ran for his life. I put my feet up on my trusty office desk and wondered how much longer I would have life as a superintendent.

11

WELCOME TO WASHINGTON

Shortly after alienating the Harrisburg establishment, I traveled with a small group of colleague superintendents from Delaware County (PA) to Washington, D.C., for an upclose and personal visit to the U.S. Office of Education. We were supposed to have an exchange of ideas. It was late October of 1988.

I should have known there would be trouble when the Washington bureaucrats all sat clustered in the front of the meeting room while the visiting superintendents occupied the audience chairs. We hadn't even yet met our hosts, and the atmosphere was already hostile.

A bald-headed, pompous twit introduced himself with some meaningless title of self-importance. He then proceeded to deliver a lengthy lecture to our group on the massive failure of America's public schools. Sort of like telling a bunch of Catholic priests that Catholicism sucks. Basically, this was the evolving rhetoric of the Reagan administration those days, with restructuring, vouchers, choice, and privatization as the buzz words to make the news media salivate and regurgitate.

This department of education official also told us that administrators were a blob that was suffocating public schools. The fool was reciting the absurd propaganda of his agency, the U.S. Office of Education. This giant federal bureaucracy had been telling America's citizenry that there was a glut of school administrators. The news media had subsequently proliferated this wisdom. Except that the U.S. Bureau of Labor Statistics showed that public education was hardly overstaffed with managerial employees when compared with business and industry. The reality is that in a typical public school, a principal might easily have sixty or more employees to monitor and evaluate. Such a supervisory work load would rarely if ever be allowed in the private sector. So much for the credibility of the U.S. Office of Education.

Anyway, we were scolded for being school administrators, just feathering our own nests and never caring about teaching or learning. Just great! We traveled all the way to the nation's capital to be belittled and insulted by this moron!

The Q and A period arrived. I was more than a little peeved. So I asked this creep what experience he had inside public schools since he was issuing such broad-based condemnations. He told us that he had been a teacher and a headmaster of a private school for ten years and that was where he learned about true quality. That and only that was his barometer! Give me a break. No experience at all with public education, yet this weasel was issuing a blatant vilification of all 87,000 public schools in the nation. This could make sense only in Washington, D.C.

I had had enough of this garbage. I requested permission to ask a very important question. "Where exactly did you park your rocket ship?" I politely inquired. The Department of Education bureaucrats looked at me in stunned silence. So did my colleagues who were wondering if my brain had collapsed. I let a few awkward moments go by and then continued. "Your rocket ship. Where the hell is it? You have just made some of the dumbest and most clueless statements I've ever heard. It's clear to me that you know nothing about who we are, what public schools are all about, or what we're trying to do. It's very obvious to me that you're an alien. Please tell us whether you're from Mars or Venus. Not that any of us really care."

The pompous twit's face was bright crimson. His colleagues squirmed. So did mine. The Martian exploded. "Fascists! Fascists! You're all fascists," he screamed as he jumped up from his chair with his arms flailing, and the professional demeanor of an out of control chimpanzee. "You school superintendents are the blob that's destroying America's schools. That's why you must be stopped and we will do it!"

I thought seriously about punching out the little twerp. I jumped up, but was restrained by a dozen sets of superintendents' arms. The room was in chaos. The two sides were yelling at one another. There was some mild pushing and shoving. To think I was paying federal taxes to support this kind of idiocy. I thought about joining the Montana Militia.

Security guards entered the room and stepped between the warring parties. More angry words. Our group was escorted from the building. Gee, does this kind of thing happen regularly here at the U.S. Office of Education?

Our gang of evil superintendents headed back to our hotel by subway. For a few minutes, we sat amidst the capital commuters in silence. Then, one of our group simply burst out laughing, obviously reliving the absurdity of a few minutes earlier. Suddenly, all of our delegation was roaring. Then the passengers on the subway joined us in laughter, although they had no idea what was so funny. As we exited the train, one passenger said that we were better than professional comedians. "Well, actually madam, we're school superintendents," I explained. "We spread joy and good feeling everywhere we go!"

Our admiring subway riders smiled and waved goodbye. It was good to be loved by the common people, or for that matter, anyone! Our superintendent contingent hurried toward the hotel bar.

12

MY VERY OWN
DEEP THROAT

That same evening, as part of our planned itinerary, we had dinner at Washington's exclusive Republican club in a private room. Very impressive. I was seated with a powerful GOP congressman. The politician's hair was professionally done, and he wore a hand-tailored silk suit. Our federal tax dollars at work.

Early on, the conversation was formal and stiff. The representative offered some prepared commentary in a brief, pre-dinner speech. We all applauded politely. Eventually the food arrived. More serious drinking progressed. By dinner's end the congressman was slightly tipsy. His tongue had come loose and he was very talkative. I was sitting next to him and we got on famously, talking about kings and queens and pussy cats. Frivolous nonsense!

It had been a long day. Most of our group bid adieu and returned to our hotel. On a hunch, I hung around. Sure enough, the congressman invited me to have a cigar with him in the adjoining smoking room full of sofas and armchairs. I decided to get heavy.

"Congressman, it seems that there's an awful lot of negative vibes about public education coming out of Washington," I began cautiously. "We've heard that much of the hostility is coming from the Reagan administration, and today our superintendents' group got a nasty dose of it at the Department of Education. I don't understand this. Most of the people in my school system, and in other school districts with which I'm familiar, are really trying to do their best. They should be getting support, not criticism."

CHAPTER 12

"Boy, I'm gonna explain all of this to you, and you probably aren't going to like any of it. So just forget where you heard it 'cause if I have to, I'll deny on a stack of Bibles that I ever even met you." The congressman spoke in a hushed voice. "Powerful people close to the president are gonna make life hell for public school folks in the years ahead. Some of them want to privatize the schools. Plenty of corporate interest here. There's gobs of money to be made if this happens.

"Others among them are into getting money away from public schools and into private and parochial schools. Then there's those that don't give a damn about schools or reform or whatever, but ripping public education is a great platform if you ain't got nothin' else. Best way to grab headlines. Best way to become important. Utter sweet nothings about schools. Bash the teacher unions. You can't miss with that stuff.

"And finally, there's some right-wing nut cases who believe that public education is godless and immoral. I'm tellin' you, boy, that these different groups in combination are gonna kick your public school teeth in. If I were you, I'd look for a different profession."

I puffed on my cigar. My yearly quota of one! I was starting to turn green. I couldn't figure out if the cigar or this pufferbelly legislator was making me sick.

"Congressman, don't you think the tidal wave you just described might be bad for the country?" I inquired. "Some people around the world think we have the best system of education anywhere because we try to teach everybody and do a pretty good job of it. Why tear apart something that works?"

"Politics is all about bein' on the power train, boy," the politician replied. "Right or wrong don't enter into this. The train I just told you about is leaving the station. I'm gettin' on board. Because the way I see it, you either get on the train or you get buried.

"Public education is headed for nothing but trouble. Boy, this is not rocket science. You get on the train or you get outta the way. That's the best free advice anyone's ever given you in your life."

His monologue left me numb. For one of the few times in my life I had nothing to say. I shook hands with my newly found deep throat and left. I decided to walk to the hotel. This was like a bad dream. What if what this congressman said was the truth? The American people had landslided Ronald Reagan and a Republican Congress into office. George Bush looked to be a lock to succeed Reagan. And this was their agenda item, to destroy public education? Who'd believe it? This was chilling stuff. I felt dirty. I needed a shower to wash off the Washington crud.

13

THE ATTEMPTED MURDER

Well, it all happened as the windy politician had predicted. And the attempted murder of public education across America is well documented. Two of the best summaries are *The Manufactured Crisis* by David Berliner and Bruce Biddle and *Setting The Record Straight* by Gerald Bracey. Both books describe an era of misinformation and misdirection and often outright lies to the American people about the status of public education across the nation.

Adolf Hitler once wrote that, "The great masses of the people will more easily fall victims to a big lie than a small one!" The führer would have been proud of so many of our elected and appointed federal government officials during the late 1980s and early 1990s here in the United States. The fabrications of these responsible persons about public education were whoppers.

Tragically, the vast majority of the American people have never heard of the *Sandia Report*. And that is as our "big brother" government in Washington decided it would be. The American people were never to learn of this 1992 analysis because its research findings countered the negative propaganda about America's public schools that had been spewed out by the Reagan and Bush hucksters.

What happened here would be funny, if it weren't so pathetically dishonest. A Bush cabinet official, trying to help the president's re-election campaign, commissioned another study of American education by a credible institution. But the results came back with the wrong answers. Wrong, that is, from our government's point of view. The extensive research findings showed that public schools across the United States were doing a pretty decent job. The White House went into a panic. The Sandia researchers and scientists were actually threatened by cabinet officers. "You bury this, or we will bury you!"

Despite the best efforts of your government and mine to cover it up, the *Sandia Report* finally found its way out of the closet in 1993. In the midst of all of the vilification of public education nationally, the Sandia National Laboratories, a federal institution of impeccable reputation, dropped these bombs on the education critics in Washington via the most comprehensive study of public education in modern times. Here are some summary points:

1. Much of the current rhetoric claims "total system-wide failure" in public education. The Sandia research shows this is simply not true.
2. Dramatic demographic changes have made the job of public schools extremely difficult. One-third of their pupils are minorities. And five million children of immigrant parents will enter schools in the 1990s.
3. Much of the nonproductive rhetoric concerning education today is based on improper use of statistics or simplistic analysis of data.
4. Many of those closely involved with international competitiveness have used the educational system to cover up their own inefficiency.

So where was *60 Minutes* on this one? Or for that matter any other major news media? Honest researchers at the Sandia Labs tragically lost their jobs because their statistical findings didn't please the Bush administration. The American people deserved to hear about this. That is what a free press is for. Is anyone out there in the news media listening?

The era of the "Big Lie" that spanned much of my career as a school superintendent was truly reprehensible. It was impossible to ignore it. It pervaded the existence of every American citizen watching television or reading a newspaper in their homes. And it slandered everyone and anyone connected with public education. Originated mostly by Washington sewer rats and their corporate allies, the untruth was given unquestioned veracity by the news media which spread it without any questions. It demoralized teachers and administrators. It gave ammunition to right-wing loonies and self-serving taxpayer groups. It jaded the thinking of many open-minded politicians and business leaders who might have lent vital support to the mission of public schools. It turned many parent supporters into doubters. It damaged public schools and the children they serve big-time. But it did not destroy them.

Frosty Troy, the editor of the *Oklahoma Observer* and a staunch defender of public education, has written suggestively that Dante on a return to earth would establish a new ring in hell for those who have attempted to obliterate public education. He calls it the most lied-about, misreported story in America. Unfortunately, giving these perpetrators their well-deserved inferno can never undo the human damage they wrought.

14

THE PRIVATE SECTOR
AS THE MODEL OF
EXCELLENCE

In 1983, just prior to my becoming a superintendent of schools, the National Commission on Excellence in Education initiated a tidal wave of public school bashing with its report *A Nation At Risk*. Within two years of the issuance of this document, more than three hundred investigative studies of public education had occurred across America. Condemnations of public schools were rampant.

One prevalent idea was that public schools were unilaterally responsible for the bleak U.S. economy and that international business and industry competitors from Asia and Europe were beating America for one reason—Asia and Europe had better schools. This was a nonsensical notion. But business and government officials pushed the idea hard. Some analysts have argued that these critics of public schools were simply scapegoating public schools to cover up the job they themselves weren't getting done.

For most of my tenure as superintendent, business and government officials perpetuated the fairy tale of public education failure. The news media carried literally hundreds of negative pieces about public schools with these private sector authority figures giving credence to the flawed theory. It didn't take long for most Americans to believe it.

However, just reflect for a moment on what subsequently transpired. Throughout most of the 1990s, the American economy reversed its fortunes and performed quite well. The U.S. stock market was bullish for most of the decade. U.S. companies were once again world-class players to be contended with by overseas competitors. So you have to wonder if America's failing public schools had somehow now become the best in the world.

In all fairness, shouldn't we apply the big business prevailing argument? The private sector had created its mythological logic of the late 1980s and early 1990s, which viewed economic success in the corporate sector as directly related to the quality of public schools. So now shouldn't America's schools be given all of the credit for the private sector's tremendous economic success during the 1990s? Not surprisingly, there has been and continues to be only silence from private and political sectors on this matter these days. And that's because these private sector experts have grown very long noses. The real culprit of the economic downturns of the 1980s had little to do with public schools, and much more to do with the management decisions at the company level and monetary, trade, and economic policies at the federal government level.

In the fall of 1988, I was invited to give a speech to a Greater Philadelphia business forum at a large hotel in the city. The speech topic was supposed to be on how schools could better address the needs of business. Don't ask me how they got my name. Ironically, I was one of the few superintendents venturing out to defend public schools back then. So they definitely picked the wrong person.

The audience of corporate types was probably expecting me to apologize for the terrible job the public schools were doing. Many university professors and even some of my own colleagues had jumped on this popular bandwagon. I was never much of a conformist.

I began my address with friendly enthusiasm. "We are of course in an election year and one of your colleagues, a CEO from a Fortune 500 company, has just written a letter to both presidential candidates, blasting public schools for turning out such defective products." The business group nodded appreciatively. They actually thought they were going to like me. I continued. "Follow the business models of excellence. That was the eloquent message of this executive. After all, his company, like yours, expects and accepts only 100 percent defect-free parts from suppliers." The dumb crowd applauded.

What a crock! Enough baiting already! Time to lower the boom. And I did. "Well, let's see. As a superintendent of schools, how should I follow such superb corporate advice?" My tone now became more than a little bit sarcastic. "I know. I too will be a bit more selective. From now in, in my school district, I will only accept 100 percent defect-free students from the community. From now on, I will reject all children who have family problems. I will reject poor and minority children. I will reject immigrants since their mastery of English is inadequate. I will reject slow learners. I will reject sick, the weak, the handicapped, the physically abused, and the delinquent."

I let this sink in. I found out that crowds of corporate executives don't yell and shout at you when they don't like what they hear. They just murmur to each other. There was a lot of murmuring in the room. I was just getting warmed up.

"It seems to me that the corporate executive who wrote that letter to the presidential candidates needs to familiarize himself with someone named Thomas Jefferson whom he's probably never heard of." I continued on my road to private sector enlightenment.

"Jefferson advocated education for the masses. And so, in public schools we utilize Jeffersonian philosophy. We teach, care about, love, and try to make a difference for every kid that comes to us—no matter what defects they bring with them."

I was on a roll, kicking their corporate butts. "Defect-free products?" I rhetorically asked. "Are you private sector people crazy? Don't you ever get out of the suburban mansions where you live and look at American society to see what's going on out there? Of the more than forty million kids in public schools, six million have disabilities, and two million speak no English. Two million more of our students have been abused or are from neglected homes. One half million of them are homeless and an equal number come from foster care and orphanages. No country in the world does what we do in caring about and trying to make a difference for this incredibly diverse student population in our public schools."

Now the audience was quiet. Most of them were actually listening. Time for the coup de grace. "What exactly is the corporate model of excellence, anyway?" I inquired. "Is everyone out there aware that just in the past two years, 580 corporations racked up 1500 violations of federal laws! Shall I send each of you the data showing that 11 percent of America's largest companies were convicted of either bribery, criminal fraud, or illegal political contributions just this last year. And over your cocktail hour tonight, will all of you be discussing the fact that 115 of the Fortune 500 have been convicted of at least one major crime in this decade? So this is the model for America's public schools? I hardly think so!"

Enough already. They looked to be beaten up enough. Besides they might become violent after all of the abuse I heaped upon them. I spent the remainder of my address talking about the philosophies of the Benedictine monks as they apply to public schools. "Temper all things. So that the brilliant will be challenged. So that the average will not be ignored. And so that the weak will not be left behind." Just a simple modus operandi for effective public schools. And so much more relevant than anything coming out of corporate or governmental arenas those days!

When I finished the speech, there was stillness in the room. Some mild and very scattered applause ensued. Then everyone quickly left. I seriously doubt that these business types collectively or individually had ever experienced anything like me or my message. Well, it was time for their education to begin.

A year or so later, *The Wall Street Journal* was still hammering away. A supplement on education generalized a sort of report card (February 9, 1990) for public schools, citing their extraordinarily low expectations for students, passivity of pupils in all classrooms and lack of academic focus on technology or basics.

I wrote to the newspaper's editors suggesting that since the *Wall Street Journal* was now into report cards, they should issue them for all American institutions. I sarcastically urged the editors to produce another supplement, this time concentrating on corporate excellence: that is, insider trading, lying, cheating, fraud, theft, false advertising, and in many cases, lousy products and services. My letter to the editor was never printed, nor did I ever get any kind of response from the paper.

15

THE GREAT SCHOOL FUNDING DISASTER

The school board was engrossed in a night of mundane discussions about instructional technology, in-service workshops and strategic curriculum planning. Members stared listlessly at each other, at their paperwork, at the piles of charts and proposals sitting before them. Then a man popped out of his chair. First, he accused the State of Pennsylvania of deliberate underfunding of public school children. He attacked the State's funding policy as an unconscionable, immoral scam. A maverick board member? Hardly. An irate taxpayer? Not quite. This flame thrower was Upper Darby's school superintendent, Joe Batory! In an age when school superintendents measure their words with the caution a driver education student shows behind the wheel, this guy prides himself on bluntness, regardless of the sting. It's a professional risk he's been willing to take.

The Philadelphia Inquirer
January 29, 1995

Exactly when I became such an outspoken lunatic, I'm really not sure. Maybe it just came naturally given the outrageous anti–public school garbage flowing out of Washington during the initial stages of my career as a superintendent. From 1985 to 1990, I wrote numerous op-ed articles and gave many fiery speeches defending public schools. It wasn't fun. Often I got hit back in public. Too many of my colleagues stayed silent, protecting their livelihoods. And the large professional public education associations, which might have made a significant difference in confronting all of this, needed hefty doses of Viagra. Unfortunately, it wasn't yet invented.

In reality, however, all of those emotional philosophical treatises I authored in response to the anti–public education propaganda out of Washington, D.C., were really mild compared with my reactions and position papers when the State of Pennsylvania stopped adequately funding public education in the early 1990s. Governor Robert Casey and his Democrat majority in the legislature essentially scrapped the state's funding plan for public education. It was an economic disaster for schools and children.

This ESBE (Equalized Subsidy for Basic Education) funding formula had used factors of student enrollment and community wealth to determine each school system's annual subsidy from the state. If a school district's pupil population was growing, it could expect increased aid from the commonwealth. How much depended on how rich or poor the school system was. This fair and equitable formula had served Pennsylvania's public schools quite well for as long as I could remember. Now the formula was no more, and school districts would have to depend on the whims of Harrisburg politicians for annual subsidies.

For three consecutive years, in spite of booming enrollment growth, the Upper Darby School District state subsidies were now frozen. Spin doctors in Harrisburg told us our governor's funding strategy was progressive. More accurately, it was brutally destructive, bringing my already financially needy school system to its knees.

In political terms, Casey was engaging in basic cost-shifting. Millions of dollars that the previous state funding formula would have generated in financial partnership to help school systems with increasing enrollments were withheld. For example, in 1992–93, twenty-eight of the thirty fastest-growing school districts in Pennsylvania had their state subsidies frozen. The commonwealth saved a bundle. But this practice also made a mockery of the Pennsylvania Constitution, which specifically mandates that the state "maintain and support a thorough and efficient system of public education."

Harrisburg now had a different priority: To remove any possibility of Pennsylvania having to implement increases in its state income tax rate, which ironically was one of the lowest in the nation. Destroying the ESBE funding formula forced conscientious school boards throughout the commonwealth to increase local property taxes if they had financial needs in their school systems or, in more simple terms, if they cared about children and public schools. The Pennsylvania School Boards Association estimated that more than one billion dollars had to be generated by school boards at the local level to make up for this state inadequacy in funding its public schools.

All of this could not have occurred at a worse time for the Upper Darby School District. Our school population was growing rapidly. We needed state help more than ever. Instead, my school system was denied millions of dollars of state aid that we would have received under the former funding system. But Pennsylvania was no longer in partnership with its public schools.

Not unlike so many other school districts across Pennsylvania, Upper Darby real estate owners got clobbered with higher property taxes in subsequent years as my school boards reluctantly did the right thing. At least we had some moral commitment to educating our community's children.

It's hard to say whether the press was stupid or incompetent or just fast asleep. In-depth analysis of the destruction of the long-standing Pennsylvania funding formula (ESBE) and its true impact on schools and taxpayers has never received adequate news media attention. The press failed miserably on this one! It's a very nasty story that never got adequately told. All the public saw was that school boards were raising taxes. Not surprisingly, citizen hostility toward public education soared to all-time heights.

16

DEMOCRAT OR REPUBLICAN? WHAT'S THE DIFFERENCE?

When I was galloping along my warpath of rage against the Democrat Bob Casey, my nine Republican school board members often joined me in criticizing the governor. The rhetoric against Casey from our board table was often white hot. What was odd though was that the three elected state representatives from our area, all Republicans elected by Upper Darby's overwhelming GOP voting majority, generally avoided any staunch support for the school district's opposition to the inadequate funding from the state's Democrat leadership. Hardly a word in anger was spoken by any of our Upper Darby state representatives against a governor from the enemy political party who was literally killing their school community with his funding policy.

Over time, I wondered if Casey's destruction of the ESBE school funding formula had Republican concurrence. Hardly shocking in Pennsylvania politics. Could some sort of deal have been cut on this? It definitely made self-serving sense for the legislators involved.

Not raising taxes at the state level was all that mattered to politicians, Democrat or Republican. Could it be that the Republican legislators were in concurrence with the Democrat Governor Casey for their own personal interests, protecting their lifetime jobs in Harrisburg? On the surface, these legislators were heroes, not needing to raise taxes at the state level. Let the school boards increase real estate taxes to keep the schools afloat and take all the heat. It was an absolutely brilliant strategy. And it victimized school districts big-time!

Any doubt I may have had about this incestuous relationship theory of Harrisburg politicians was quickly put aside when Republican Tom Ridge was swept into the Pennsylvania governor's chair in 1994. That's because nothing changed. The state's share of basic education funding continued to decline under the Ridge administration to its lowest levels ever. And the Upper Darby School District, like many others, staggered on fiscally because of its continuing surge of pupil enrollment, which state subsidies continued to ignore.

Beyond inadequately funding the public schools, Governor Ridge also brought a bag of "party line" agenda goodies with him into office. This man definitely wanted to be vice president. He knew what he had to do. Vouchers and charter schools were now the priorities for Pennsylvania, although this was hardly the popular sentiment of the Commonwealth's citizenry. And in heavily Republican Upper Darby a new commandment was issued: "Thou shalt not criticize our beloved Republican Governor!"

Obedience was never one of my virtues. When nothing changed for the better after the first year of the Republican Ridge as Governor, I lashed out with another of my tirades. Ridge was little more than another Bob Casey. He continued to underfund public education statewide. Equal time for all governors is what I advocate! I decided to go after Ridge.

In a lightweight platform statement of February 6, 1996, Ridge revealed his blueprint for the future to his fellow Pennsylvanians. I think I publicly referred to it as a blueprint for disaster, especially regarding public schools. All four newspapers on the school district beat reported my comments. I was quickly put on Republican hit lists!

Shortly thereafter, as the chairperson of Delaware County's superintendents' group, I was invited to testify before a bipartisan subcommittee of Pennsylvania legislators who were allegedly studying the state's funding system for public education. By this time, I had a reputation as a troublemaker. Several of my nervous colleagues had expressed concern that I not alienate these elected officials. Oh sure! These elected officials had frozen most of the school district subsidies in Delaware County for three consecutive years, and I was supposed to bend over and thank them. No chance! I delivered my insanity message as part of my commentary. It truly fit the times.

"Honored legislators," I stated with great humility before these royals. "It is with extreme gratitude that I acknowledge your willingness to address the insanity issue in Harrisburg. It is my sincere hope that this problem is not based in mental disorder, but rather in misdirection.

"Whatever the case, this insanity is a fever caused by false economy. Save a few bucks now. Pay for it later." The legislators were beginning to understand that I was a problem child. I could see in their faces that some of them were even wondering if I had escaped from some asylum and was impersonating a superintendent.

I continued to plummet downward. "This is not a good strategy for an enlightened commonwealth regarding the children who attend its public schools. And yet two governors, one Democrat and now a Republican, have been afflicted by the insanity. Indeed, this abdication of funding responsibility by Harrisburg has alas made me somewhat insane as well. And so it is my sincere hope that the legislature will cure this insanity. The antidote is right before your eyes. Simply, bring back the ESBE formula to reinstitute fair and equitable funding of Pennsylvania's public schools. Thank you."

The legislators on the subcommittee just ogled me. They surely figured that I was crazy. But, like foxes, they were too smart to bite my hooks. I was spoiling for a fight. A good debate. The minority Democrats seemed to smirk. The Republican majority glared at me with contempt. I had said something bad about their beloved governor. Silence ensued. The chairperson firmly said thank you. I was summarily dismissed.

In the backrooms where Upper Darby's local political leaders and state representatives made the real decisions, all hell broke loose. My sarcastic comments about inadequate state subsidies for public schools were incendiary to the Republican power structure since they now had control of both the governor's chair and both legislative chambers. The conclusions of these politicians were uniformly firm: Batory had to go.

I ignored the writing on the wall. I'll leave when I'm ready to leave! From 1996 until I retired in 1999, I endured lots of icy treatment, cold-shoulders, and cheap-shots behind my back from local politics in Upper Darby. A good school superintendent often has to be tough and solitary especially where principle is involved. I had stood up for my community's public schools and the students that attended them. That was what mattered. And I could have cared less about the Emperor Ridge and his aspirations for the White House. To this day, my wife, Joan, marvels at how well I slept at night during those difficult times. I had walked on a political cliff for the first twelve years of my career as a superintendent. Then I stepped over the edge. But I didn't fall. In my last three years, I may have been a political wallflower, but I liked it much better.

17

THE TAXPAYER
GROUP BLOODBATH

In the fall of 1995, my nine-member school board and I were in attendance at a seminar on public relations at the University of Pennsylvania. School budget season every spring was becoming more and more difficult. We were trying to learn how to improve our situation. A distinguished professor from the Wharton School was offering his advice to a large gathering of public school officials via a prepared speech.

"Reach out to the public. Engage them. Involve them. Trust them. Even your worst adversaries." He concluded with enthusiasm. "If you let them into the process, if you remove the darkness from your deliberations, they will become an asset. They will make your tasks that much easier. Openness and trust must become your tools."

The audience applauded appreciatively. I could see my school board was impressed. I smelled trouble. The regular adversaries at our school board meetings didn't seem to me to be hoping for a chance to help us. They were always trying to destroy us. Reach out to them? I'd like to kill most of them!

Sure enough, several months later, as budget preparations for the next school year had just gotten underway, my school board, remembering the wisdom of the university sage they had recently heard, decided on full disclosure. Before we rolled up our sleeves to effect any real economies and prior to the annual paring down of preliminary budgetary requests from a hundred sources, we went public with our preliminary expenditure needs for the next school year. We informed the small group of citizens that frequented our public meetings that we would welcome their input and suggestions and ideas.

We needed and wanted their help. We would get through these difficult times together in our new age of cooperativeness. The first budget planning session was scheduled for our administration building in about a week. The age of enlightenment had arrived.

Four days later, literally thousands of flyers were inserted under the windshield wipers of cars parked in Upper Darby's three major shopping centers.

It's Time To Fight Back!!!!!!!!!!

The Upper Darby School Board and its spend-crazy Superintendent of Schools have gone too far. They are ready to impose new real estate tax increases that will drive good and decent hard-working people out of their homes.

Don't let them get away with this. Join us at the public meeting this coming Wednesday at the Upper Darby School District Administration Building at 8:00 P.M.

This irresponsible School Board will be stopped, and we will lead the fight. But we need you to be there with us. A large crowd will show them that we mean business.

The Newly Formed
Upper Darby Association
To Stop Tax Increases!

On Wednesday evening, forty-five minutes before our first budget session was to get underway, the boardroom was packed. It was a surly and ugly group of several hundred citizens, loaded for bear. At the building entrance and stretching along the sidewalks outside were several hundred more residents who were now "ticked off" because they couldn't get inside the overflowing building.

I conferenced with the school board leadership. We made some quick phone calls and arranged to move the meeting to a large school auditorium facility nearby. My board president announced the move to the packed house. Something whizzed by his head. What the hell was that? I looked at the wall behind the board table and saw a splattered grape. At least it wasn't a bullet hole. I began bobbing and weaving my head Southwest Philly style. Hitting a moving target is always much harder. Another grape sped by! The curses and shouts and threats continued, although I didn't notice any more grape shots. Lots of people with red faces. Finally, the angry crowd swarmed out of the administration building headed for the new meeting location.

This was not a situation for the weak of heart. I made a quick phone call to our township police captain. He said he would try to get some presence over to the school, but all of their officers were on assigned duty in the neighborhoods. He couldn't promise anything. The school board and I followed the mob out the door to the new meeting destination, our death chamber.

Estimates of the crowd assembled at the Drexel Hill Middle School ranged from seven hundred to nine hundred people. Considering that a typical school board meeting averaged about thirty attendees, this was just a bit frightening. Joy of joys, though. Two of Upper Darby's finest were in the back of the auditorium. I felt much safer!

We all stood and recited the Pledge of Allegiance. And then my board president, a devout Catholic who was somewhat unnerved, offered a lengthy prayer beseeching Jesus Christ to help us. Obviously, he was near the edge. The rest of the board members and I bowed our heads like we were in church. Interesting, since we had never before had a prayer before any public meeting. In addition, the invocation wasn't very ecumenical. Perhaps our prayerful leader would correct that with his benediction. Of course, issuing bulletproof vests might have been a better idea.

One of the first speakers appeared to be drunk. Believe it or not, he was a refined business executive during the daytime. But his moon was out tonight. He rambled on and cursed frequently. His message was incoherent. The board president tried to get him under control. No chance. Jesus wasn't answering prayer requests tonight! The tirade went on. The crowd was hooting and hollering. The two outmanned Upper Darby cops showed courage under fire. They escorted the maniac out of the auditorium in the face of real danger. The mob loudly expressed its disapproval.

It was all uphill after that. One of the longest, never-ending hills I've ever been on. The newly formed taxpayers group leaders each made biting statements, citing our financial incompetence. Many first time visitors jumped on their bandwagon. A number of senior citizens rambled on about their dire financial situations. Just a minute here! If they want to see real money trouble, they should try running a school district.

Basically, we got scorched. We listened attentively as we always did. Most of the board members took notes. I just stared. Our board president spokesperson tried to explain that any thoughts about the size of a tax increase were very preliminary at this early stage of the budget process. The audience booed him and shouted him down. I thought about Penn professors and governors and firing squads.

One of the taxpayer group ringleaders got his turn at the microphone and targeted me. Of all things, this was a guy I had helped to find employment when he was out of work. His gratitude was overwhelming.

"This meeting has been going on for more than one hour, and I haven't heard the superintendent of schools say one intelligent thing," he challenged. "It's obvious he's not even listening to us." The crowd roared its approval. It set off my damn fuse.

"Actually, sir, I have been paying very close attention to everything that has been said to this point here this evening," I responded. "It's just that I haven't heard one intelligent thing said by anyone, including you. So, there's really nothing for me to say. It's really pathetic that not one person in this audience has mentioned the children of this community and the need to have good schools for them."

I would have continued, but the board members seated on each side of me were simultaneously pinching my thighs from opposite sides. It hurt like hell. It also meant *shut the hell up,* so I did. Arms and fists were raised in the audience. New decibel level records for this auditorium were established. Well, there! Who said I wasn't paying attention? The abuse continued onward and upward until after midnight.

When the meeting was finally over, I headed for the side entrance of the Drexel Hill Middle School. I thought I might slip out amid the crowd. No such luck. I walked right into a macho male group of taxpayers milling around the exit.

One of them shouted at me. I had visions of the Ox Bow incident! "Just who do you think you are! We pay your salary. You can't talk to us like you did. We're not gonna take it!" Somebody call a timeout! I had been listening to this crap for four hours. I just wanted to go home. I didn't feel like fighting anymore. I was exhausted.

And then miracle of miracles. Rocco and two of his soldiers stepped out of the shadows. Rocco made a brief announcement: "Joey, you're goin' home. Youse smacks, get outta the way before you get hurt!" I thought Rocco's directions were very clear.

But one naive taxpayer moron didn't get the message. "You don't scare us. You can't order us around!" This statement was not very bright.

Rocco walked over to the lynch mob. He pulled up an inch or two from the loud-mouthed taxpayer's face. He looked him in the eyes. Then he said very quietly, "You talkin' to me? I don't think so. What I do think is that you're a first-class wimp who better get outta here before I break your bones!"

By this time, Rocco's two men had pulled me away and were escorting me out the door and to my car. Dammit, I wanted to see more of the confrontation. I thought it was really unfair. Only ten of them against Rocco. They might all get killed. It made me tingle with joy!

In the days and weeks and months and years that followed, I spent a great deal of time mobilizing parents and teachers and administrators in support of our schools. I met with every home and school association and all school district union leaders. I cajoled them. I challenged them. If they didn't care, who would or should?

To hell with the University of Pennsylvania's Wharton School and its ivory-tower, conciliatory philosophies. We were in a war. From now on, we would fight back. No more pretending. Us against them! At first, small contingents from our schools began to regularly engage the malcontents in public debate. Later, a very large previously silent majority became eloquent and formidable. Our advocates demanded that the missing part of the equation— teaching and learning and students—be prioritized in the financial discussions. What an unusual idea.

Through much of these difficult times, I was a lightning rod for attackers. The plight of any school superintendent who dares to not hide in the closet. Only now, when people took shots in the press or at public meetings, I fired back. I torched more than a few citizen enemies with a scathing tongue. A good superintendent of schools stands up when he or she has to. First and foremost, you don't back off from bullies trying to destroy public schools.

Parents and teachers and administrators and school board members regularly rallied around me. We fought a hundred pitched battles in various public forums. It was guerrilla warfare. Slowly but surely, the taxpayer group finally disintegrated. Reach out to them? What the hell for? They were never interested in common ground. They deserved to die, and we vanquished them. At the budget hearing and board budget vote meetings in June of 1999, just three years after the taxpayer group had peaked in size and ugliness, a grand total of three persons from our community of 85,000 spoke against the budget. What taxpayer group? One of my greatest triumphs!

18

LESSONS ABOUT PUBLIC EDUCATION FROM VIETNAMESE AMERICANS

The best thing that happened in the Upper Darby School District during my term of office as superintendent was the influx of Vietnamese. In no way do I want to slight the fifty other first-generation nationalities that were circulating through my school district while I presided, but the Vietnamese were the majority of the minorities, and so I've focused on them to drive home a point. What public schools do so very well!

The Vietnamese newcomers to the Upper Darby School District settled into a neighborhood just across the borderline from Philadelphia. They had little money, but they brought with them the very best values that most of us like to think of as American. They prioritized hard work, family, and education as keys to success. The formula for the American Dream as it's served so many previous generations. And these newest Americans had it down to a science. Their children became superb school citizens and students because this was what was expected and demanded from the home. And they excelled.

The first Vietnamese to reside in Upper Darby did not exactly find the promised land. Asian American gangs from outside of Upper Darby preyed on them. The gangsters knew that these newest arrivals in America had been conditioned in Vietnam not to trust banks or police. That meant two things: Money would be kept in their Upper Darby homes, not in banks; and these newcomers would not readily call Upper Darby police since their experience with police in Vietnam equated with corruption.

For many months, Vietnamese homes in Upper Darby were invaded by hooligans in the wee hours of the night. With enough threats and sometimes physical abuse, whatever money these immigrants had earned was surrendered to the crooks. The Vietnamese were unlikely to call the police, but to make sure, the gangsters promised to return and cut the throats of all family members if any contact was made with law enforcement authorities. How many of these robberies actually occurred is difficult to document because of the imposed silence that followed the crimes. Eventually, the Upper Darby police, to their credit, cracked the scam and made numerous arrests. Much of this finally happened because of Hao, a gentlemanly Vietnamese-American Upper Darby resident, who painstakingly convinced many of his former countrymen to utilize banks and trust the police.

Hao became one of the first Asian Americans elected to anything in Delaware County, and he served on the Upper Darby School Board for several years. He was a valuable asset to me, a superb resource on all things Asian. He also became my good friend. Hao and I once went to a Philadelphia Phillies baseball game at Veteran's Stadium as guests of one of the school district's vendors. I looked forward to enlightening Hao about the finer points of the game. I would show him my vast knowledge of America's pastime.

In the first inning with a New York Met's runner on first base, Hao screamed out to me and everyone around us, "I've stolen the sign. He's gonna try to steal second!" Sure enough, the Met broke with the pitch and slid safely into second base. From that point on, it was Hao who was incessantly pointing out to me the idiosyncrasies of baseball as we enjoyed the game together. Hao never ceased to amaze me in everything he did.

The Little Saigon restaurant is a small family-operated business in the 69th Street section of Upper Darby. The Vietnamese chef and owner, Edward, prepares the freshest and most delicious fare this side of Ho Chi Minh City. Edward is a delightful conversationalist.

He'll tell you of his upbringing in a Buddhist monastery, his eventual flight from Vietnam, and his arrival in the United States with nothing but hope. He's also the best advertisement for public education I could ever hope to produce. No less than twenty-three members of Edward's family—uncles, aunts, nieces, nephews, cousins, his children and theirs—have gone through the Upper Darby schools in recent years. All either have advanced degrees or are currently in college.

Now if public education is broken as so many of its naysayers would have the general public believe, what are we then to make of the success stories of Edward's family? For many of these young people, English was not even their first language. How could they possibly go on to such success in higher education utilizing a broken public school system? I once asked Edward about the remarkable academic achievements of his family members in Upper Darby's schools, and he explained it all very succinctly: A matter of priorities. Family, education, and diligence. All at the very top of the list in Vietnamese American households.

Jesse Jackson once said, "America has always been about opportunity and never about guarantees." Public schools are the classic example of this. Those students who prioritize education and work at it, sooner or later succeed. And it's been that way for a very long time in Upper Darby and across America whether kids are recent immigrants or can trace their lineage to the Mayflower. Broken? Hardly. Public education has always been and continues to be a remarkably effective institution for those who opt to take advantage of the marvelous opportunities it provides.

Minh was a delicate Vietnamese flower who arrived in my broken and ineffective school system as an eighth grader. She spoke no English. Five years later, in 1995, she was graduated number one in the class academically. Minh took more college-level advanced placement courses at Upper Darby High School than any previous student in history. She was granted status as a junior upon entering Penn State University in the pre-med program of studies. She was graduated magna cum laude in two years.

At Philadelphia's Thomas Jefferson Medical School, despite being chronologically much younger than her peers, Minh ranked near the top academically among all medical students. But she was not number one! Minh apologized for this failing to me in writing. She also clearly identified my broken educational system as the key to her academic success. But, then, what does Minh know? There are so many self-anointed experts in America who know so much better. Or do they?

As a kid, I had made a vow to myself that I would never forget being poor. And that if I ever got anywhere financially, I would try to help others. One of the ways I kept this promise was to establish a personally funded scholarship at our senior high school shortly after I became superintendent. The specifications that I gave the high school were that the kid need money and have academic promise. Based on those criteria, the high school could pick the recipient. I wanted no part in the selection process.

In late May of 1985, it was Senior Awards Night at Upper Darby High School. Students getting scholarships and other awards were invited along with their parents and others. The seniors arrived dressed better that I had ever seen them. They sat surrounded by their smiling families in our huge auditorium. A gala evening.

I was seated on the stage next to my high school principal, Gil, and the other scholarship/award presenters. Giving my own scholarship—a natural high. I beamed with pride. A real ego trip for yours truly.

The ceremonies progressed. Kids came up to get awards. Cheers, tears, and joy! I couldn't wait to hand out my scholarship. Finally, they called the name of my winner. She wasn't there. Awkward silence. I stood in front of everyone like an idiot. My moment in the sun ruined. The program went on. Someone was going to pay for my humiliation! I was furious.

"Gil, I'm not sure if you're going to be working here in the future," I angrily told my high school principal when the festivities ended. "But on the chance that you would like to continue onward and upward in your career, I strongly suggest that you have an explanation of this farce to me by 8:00 A.M. tomorrow." The only "no show" of the entire evening turned out to be my scholarship recipient. How could this have happened?

Gil called me at my office at 7:30 A.M. the next morning. "Can you come over to see me?" he asked. "I've got the answer to last night, and I can't do it justice over the phone." I told Gil I was on the way.

Five minutes later, I entered the high school principal's office. Gil was behind his desk. A Vietnamese teenager was seated on his couch. It was obvious that she had been crying. "Amy, please tell the superintendent what you told me earlier this morning," Gil directed.

"I am so very sorry that I have hurt you. This I never meant to do. I have already received so much goodness from the Upper Darby High School," Amy sobbed. "My parents and I did not understand how I could be worthy of such an important award from our most honorable superintendent. We were certain there was some mistake. I was too embarrassed to even mention this to my teachers or friends. I thought that they would laugh at my pride in thinking that I might be considered for such an honor. Now this morning, I have found that it is all true, that I was supposed to receive a scholarship. What you must think of me. I have done something unforgivable. I am so unworthy."

By this time, Gil and I were each emotional basket cases. Two crumbled tough guys. Nobody spoke for awhile. I went over to the sofa and sat down beside Amy. I handed her a tissue and told her to wipe her eyes. I gave her my scholarship. We stood up and faced one another and did a lot of bowing. I told her she was indeed a very worthy student and that she should never forget it. I didn't tell her how unworthy I felt at that moment.

19

THE
ASSASSINATION PLOT

It really wasn't that big a thing. Early in 1992, two Asian American students from Upper Darby High School exited a bus on arriving back in their neighborhood at the end of the school day. Five thugs immediately jumped them, roughed them up, and stole about $12 from them. Neighbors called police. An investigation ensued the next day at the school.

The two ninth-grade victims told the inquiring high school administrators that the perpetrators were older students from the high school, and that they were all Greek. This was a good clue, so the senior high school investigators focused on questioning Upper Darby High students from the Greek American neighborhood in our community. That same day, five kids were apprehended, their parents were called in, and each pupil was suspended from school for ten days.

I thought that was the end of it. However, the next morning, one of our local newspapers carried a story about a gang fight among Upper Darby High School students. According to the article, the school was a tinderbox ready to explode. In reality, my best guess is that 99 percent of the three thousand pupils at the high school knew little or nothing about this episode.

I called the newspaper and complained. The editor asked whether the crime was committed by a Greek gang as the Upper Darby police had told them. I confirmed that our victims had pointed the investigators to some Greek American students who had done the deed. I was trying to be open and straightforward with the press. Bad mistake. I noted that I didn't think there was any gang involved and further suggested that this incident was a minor robbery and hardly an ethnic war. I expressed my concern that such incendiary news coverage could inflame a school where many different racial and ethnic groups lived together amicably. My comments were reported in another article a few days later. To me, the whole thing was over.

About a week later, I received an afternoon telephone call from one of my teachers. He had just returned from lunch at a local diner where he had overheard a group of parish leaders from our community's Greek Orthodox Church discussing a vicious editorial they were writing about me. He thought they were going to submit it to area newspapers. It was essentially about me being a bigot. These church leaders were vowing to destroy me in the press. I thanked the caller for the tip and hung up. I was suddenly sick to my stomach.

I immediately telephoned my next door neighbor, Dr. Nick, a close friend and prominent Greek American physician, and a member of this parish. I told him what I knew and begged for help. A few minutes later, he called me back and said that he had arranged a meeting in his home with the parish priest that afternoon.

When I was introduced to the priest in Dr. Nick's home a few hours later, I knew I was a condemned man. I groveled. I told the priest of the discrimination that my family and I had faced all our lives. How it had sensitized me to being tolerant of others.

"Father, you must believe me. I have many shortcomings as a human being, but bigotry is not one of them," I pleaded. "I would never do anything or say anything to willfully hurt Greek Americans or any other ethnic or racial group."

"My son, it is much too late for this. Whatever you are saying to me doesn't matter. Our parish council president has already sent his opinion article to the newspapers," the pastor informed me. "You seem like a sincere person, but the matter is out of my control. Whether or not I believe you is irrelevant. The parish council has decided that you are a bigot, and I will not get involved." And so, it was all moot. My heart sunk. Dr. Nick sighed and rolled his eyes. The priest left. I crawled back to my home next door in terror.

The *News of Delaware County,* our community weekly, printed the attack, and gave it prominent play (February 5, 1992) as an op-ed piece instead of the letter to the editor that it was. I was accused of "racial and ethnic slurs" against immigrants and minorities. The parish council president built his case against me on the fact that I had identified the robbers in this incident as Greek American. Yes, I had verified for the press what they already knew from other sources.

And then additional examples of my criminality were presented. In one of my transgressions from several years before, it was noted that I had denied admittance to a potential exchange student. This incident, which received extensive newspaper coverage, supposedly proved my bias toward all ethnic groups. Another of my alleged offenses was in a recent op-ed article where I had made a reference to a practice of the Japanese government. Finally, I was accused of perpetually blaming immigrants for the Upper Darby School District's low standardized test scores. Clearly, I was the bigot of all bigots!

For the record, I did in fact refuse the admittance of one exchange student in 1987. He had arrived at the school district without obtaining the required pre-approval for admittance. When my high school principal, Gil, and I finally saw the kid's application papers, we found out that he did not meet the minimum Upper Darby School District requirements for an exchange pupil. We denied entry.

Over the years, we had enrolled numerous exchange pupils from all over the world. All of them met the criteria for admittance and adhered to timelines for approval. This pupil had no chance of getting into our high school. He and his host family became community martyrs in the local press. Another case of the big bad school district beating up some poor innocent. As is typical, we avoided revealing any specific reasons for the denial of admittance. I became a villain, of course, and caught hell in several newspaper editorials.

In the op-ed piece in question, I had simply noted an article in the *Philadelphia Inquirer* (May 23, 1991), that documented the Japanese government hiring away young American science graduates from U.S. universities. I thought I made a clever rebuttal to critics of schooling in America. My point was that if education was so bad in the United States, why would Japan, the country with allegedly the best education system in the world, be aggressively recruiting products of America's inferior system of schooling. My attackers somehow deemed this to be an ethnic slur on all Japanese.

And, finally, I had always called attention to the difficulty of standardized tests for any student whose first language was not English, especially if that pupil had been in the United States for only a short time. Not exactly earth

shaking, but this variable was often ignored in administration of various testing programs. This was in fact a defense of immigrant students, not a con-
demnation.

Unfortunately, this was a kangaroo court. The newspaper conduits of this
defamation acted like Moses had just come down from the mountain with a
delicious scoop! *Superintendent of Schools as the main course of the barbecue.
Everybody take a bite!*

There are no words to adequately describe the pain and embarrassment
of being so falsely accused by the printed word. School district attorneys informed me that as a public figure, I had no legal recourse. I rejected writing
any personal rebuttal because I've never believed that strategy worked. I decided to remain silent. Somebody give me the vial of poison, please!

In all of my professional life, this was my low point. I have no idea what I
might have done without the support of my wife, Joan. I clung to her des-
perately. I retreated into a shell. It was the worst of times.

And then everything suddenly changed. Numerous letters in defense of
my character and beliefs began flowing into the newspapers from multiple
sources. Parents, teachers, administrators, community merchants, Rotary
Club members, and even some brave parishioners of this church deluged the
newspapers with letters to the editor defending my character. People knew
the real me. And they knew slander and lies when they saw them. Eventually,
the *News of Delaware County* refused to take any more letters to the editor on
my behalf. They couldn't handle the volume. It restored my faith in the
goodness of people. I got up off the deck, took the mandatory count of eight,
and got back into the fight.

20

THE HOWARD STERN AFFAIR

This one was a classic. Sometime during 1998, a tenth-grade student at Upper Darby High School was suspended for three days for making a vulgar remark in the presence of a full homeroom of peers.

The pupil and his mother vehemently protested the suspension, arguing that the young man was only parroting what was said by national radio show celebrity, Howard Stern, in one of his videos. Their appeal fell on the deaf ears of the high school administrators. So the next morning, mother and son called the Howard Stern radio show live and on the air in New York. Stern got on the line with them and promised to come to the rescue of the oppressed student and his mother with his lawyers. Our switchboard at the school district quickly lit up like a Christmas tree. Two hundred people in our community were dying to tell us that the great Howard Stern was bad-mouthing our school system on the radio at that very minute.

Later that day, a Stern staffer called me. "Howard's ready to come down there and turn you people into mincemeat. He's contacted his personal lawyer to help these people. I've never seen him so pissed off," the voice threatened. "This isn't worth all the bad publicity the school district is gonna get outta this. If you have any sense, you'll back off this kid's suspension before we deliver you a raft of shit."

"Now, understand this first and foremost. I don't give a damn about Howard Stern or anybody else in that rathole you're calling from," I flatly replied. "This kid is going to stay suspended for three days no matter what you do. What this kid did is wrong, and deserves to be treated accordingly.

Tell your boss to do what he has to do. Nobody's going to tell me how to run this school district! Tell Mr. Stern that if he shows his face in Upper Darby, he'll end up getting his clock cleaned by about thirty fathers of female students who have already told me that they don't want their daughters hearing such trash in school. I'd just love to tell them that Howard Stern is coming to town to defend the vile behavior of this young man. It's very possible Howie will be the one getting his head handed to him. So, come on down. We'll be waiting." I slammed the phone down. I was boiling. I fantasized having my hands around Stern's throat.

I never again heard from Howard Stern or his people. However, because the suspended student and his mother were overheard by so many listeners talking live on syndicated radio with Howard Stern that morning, the area news media now went ballistic. Fun and games for the feeble minded. Five Philadelphia television station crews invaded the high school campus. And all five newspapers on our beat sent reporters. It was a rotten day. We fielded their questions and held our ground. Then we threw them all off the high school campus.

The reporter and camera persons from one of the Philadelphia television stations were particularly belligerent about being ordered off the grounds. I told them that they had disrupted enough education for one day. I would have them arrested if they didn't leave. So they reluctantly left.

At 7:00 P.M. that same evening, I received a telephone call from my maintenance supervisor, Mike. The camera crew that had given me all the trouble in the morning had just tried to enter the empty high school, but had been evicted by our night cleaning workers. Next, their van had bizarrely sped around the high school building about ten times and now sat parked across the street from the high school in the cemetery. The high school was under surveillance. What was going on here? Were these people on drugs? Didn't these news media idiots have anything better to do?

My home was only eight blocks away. I walked down to the high school, and spotted the television van across the street. I came up from behind with marvelous stealth and banged on the driver side window. I scared the living daylights out of the two people inside, which was what I intended to do.

"So what's going on, fellas?" I inquired. I was attired in a leather jacket with a Boston Red Sox baseball hat pulled down over my eyes. I was doing my best imitation of Robert Parker's Spenser. "Why aren't you out filming blood and guts and body bags? This has to be pretty boring."

The reporter was not in the truck. Just two camera people. They recognized me in spite of my disguise. "You're gonna get yours tomorrow morning, wise ass," one of them responded. I must have made quite an impression earlier in the day when I ordered these morons off the high school grounds. "The word is that Howard Stern and his lawyers are going to force you to admit that suspended kid back into school tomorrow morning. He's gonna show up on your doorstep with the kid and his mom. We're just getting some footage of the high school to preview his arrival on tonight's news! You oughta watch it. It's about you. Oh, and by the way, we're on private property so mind your own goddamn business."

I thought for a split second about slugging the arrogant punk. Then, I thought about calling the cops. Instead, I walked home. I needed to think. Tomorrow was the last day of the student's suspension. Was Howard Stern nutty enough to travel down from New York to make a scene about this silly incident? How the hell did I know?

By the time morning rolled around, we were ready. I stood at the high school front door with my principal and assistant principals, two of Upper Darby's finest, and six of my biggest maintenance workers. I felt like one of those Southern demagogue governors blocking admittance to the schoolhouse. What was I doing here? We now had three television crews parked across the street along with a group of newspaper reporters and a pack of citizen gawkers waiting for the action.

Nearly three thousand pupils poured into the school as they did every morning, chirping and laughing, apathetic about the potential Gunfight at the OK Corral. And, as it turned out, all my tension was for nothing. No suspended kid, mom, or Howard Stern showed their faces. By 9:00 A.M., all the news media had disappeared. I was greatly relieved. Maybe, I could do something regarding teaching and learning today. Wouldn't that be different.

And then I spotted him around the far corner of the high school. No, not Howard Stern—it was Rocco and three of his soldiers. No nonsense guardian angels. I can only speculate on what might have happened if Howard Stern and his cronies had arrived. But I can tell you that it would have been quick and ugly. And, God, how I would have really enjoyed it. This was the biggest mistake Howard Stern never made. I do so wish he had showed up!

When all was said and done, the news coverage of this student suspension was absurdly out of proportion to reality. Granted, the notoriety of Howard Stern had a lot to do with that. The kid became a celebrity in the newspapers, and with Greater Philadelphia radio and television talking heads. Even got onto the Montel Williams' show. The kid also stayed suspended. The crisis soon died away.

21

BOOK BANNING IN THE UPPER DARBY SCHOOL DISTRICT

Inever could stand being away from the school district when I was super-intendent. I always feared the worst. One bright summer Monday, Joan and I were enjoying a vacation day at the Jersey shore. We had slept late and were lingering over coffee, something we didn't get to do often enough. I was casually paging through the *Philadelphia Inquirer* when I arrived at the editorial page and nearly had a coronary.

There right in front of my face was a huge editorial blasting the Upper Darby School District for its decision to remove *Huckleberry Finn* from all of its school library shelves. The headline read: "Huck Finn is tossed out of Upper Darby's schools, but what kind of educational standard is this?"

There was just one small problem with this editorial of four hundred words: not one word of it was true. My school district was savaged as a book banner by one of the nation's largest and most respected newspapers, but it never happened. Oh, there was such a crisis in the Upper *Dublin* School District two counties away. But it sure wasn't Upper *Darby*. I picked up my trusty weapon, the telephone, and called the *Inquirer's* editorial offices. "I'm very concerned with the drug problem at the *Inquirer*," I raged at the unfortunate editor who fielded my call. "These hallucinogenic drugs being used by your editorial writers are a real threat to your paper's existence. I demand that you do something about this problem."

The stammering editor on the other end of the line figured he had some crazy on the phone, and hoped to end the conversation by saying he'd take the matter under advisement. "Is there anything else?" he asked.

CHAPTER 21

"Actually there is! You see, I'm the superintendent of schools in the school district where your asinine editorial said that *Huckleberry Finn* was just banned. You are aware, aren't you, that this morning's editorial about book banning in the Upper Darby School District is totally untrue," I continued. "It has to be drugs that would keep an editorial writer from checking out the facts before printing the editorial. You idiots have the wrong school district. What explanation could there be other than drugs?" The editor's light bulb finally had some current.

The editor apologized and promised a retraction would be printed the next day. I told him, "Thanks for nothing!" Sure enough, the following morning, the *Inquirer* buried a one-inch retraction on its op-ed page. Newspaper justice!

22

THE WALL
STREET JOURNAL
BUTCHER JOB

A major complaint that I have with the news media these days is that the angle for the story is often determined in advance of the reporter acquiring the facts. That is a biased and backwards approach to journalism. It was never more evident than in an episode with the *Wall Street Journal* in November of 1997.

One of its reporters was sent down from the paper's headquarters to do a feature on an inner ring suburb, that is, a community that borders a large city. Someone decided that the Upper Darby School District, serving the second most densely populated community in Pennsylvania, and situated just west of Philadelphia, would be a good illustration.

But someone had also decided what an inner ring suburb should look like. The young and personable reporter asked to see streets filled with boarded-up homes and the multiple drug corners. Where were the gangs located and the graffiti-covered buildings? I didn't know where to find any of this in quantity in our community of 85,000, and I told him so.

Instead, I chauffeured the reporter all over the different neighborhoods. To his amazement I showed him a thousand leafy green properties in Drexel Hill and tons of nicely kept row houses in many parts of Upper Darby and Clifton Heights. I took him to the revitalized commercial district adjacent to Philadelphia and we ate lunch there. And we visited one of our Blue Ribbon National Schools of Excellence where student newcomers to America who have arrived from more than fifty nations predominate. I praised the work of township government, the cops, and the clergy.

CHAPTER 22

So what's the deal here? Is there something wrong with not being a wealthy, homogeneous community? Or with being largely working class, or with being multi-ethnic, or with no longer being as lily white as we once were? Who said this is equivalent to a community dying? Certainly our schools, as a source of neighborhood pride, were still our heartbeat. And our changing community had largely come to view its new diversity as an asset. So we didn't have a rich tax base. So what? We were hanging in there. The reporter seemed taken aback from whatever preconceived notions he had. We shook hands. I thought I might have headed off another news media debacle. He went back to the paper to write his story.

The article in the *Wall Street Journal* ran on Thursday, November 13, 1997. It carried sweeping generalizations about devastation and suburban decay and decline. It mentioned that Upper Darby's schools were jammed with troubled youngsters from dozens of nations. There was nothing positive about the community or the schools. Indeed, we fit the mold of one of those inner ring suburbs. It had all been decided in advance.

I went ballistic. I smashed things and cursed a blue streak. Worthless inventors of the news! In the closet of my office, I kept an inflated five-foot-tall Bugs Bunny punching bag. My nieces and nephews had given it to me for our annual Christmas Pollyanna. Everyone in the family was afraid to ask what I wanted it for. It was for emergencies like this one. I beat the living daylights out of Bugs Bunny.

Sandy was my new administrative assistant, having replaced the retired Anne. Sandy was a kind and competent angel. She heard the racket and thought I was having a seizure or being attacked by persons unknown. She courageously opened my office door and entered. It's a good thing she was used to me. The place was a wreck. Stuff was all over the floor. Some of it was broken. Bugs Bunny was deflated. He looked like he'd been steamrolled! I had killed the long-eared wabbit. I was lying on my couch exhausted.

Calmly and quietly, like nothing happened, I asked Sandy to get the *Wall Street Journal* editorial offices on the phone. She scurried out of the destroyed office. I got connected to an assistant editor. I wasn't holding together too well. I yelled and cursed and threatened everyone at the newspaper, especially the writer of the article. It just wasn't fair, I made the mistake of telling the assistant editor. He came back with the life isn't fair cliché. He was right. And fairness is definitely not a concept with which the news media is familiar.

23

THE NEWS MEDIA IS THE VOICE OF GOD AND WILL LIVE FOREVER

I remember reading a Russian author who wrote that when peasants were accosted by the Czar's troops, they would always say: "The Czar is the voice of God, and will live forever!" The translation of what the peasants really meant is that the Czar was a worthless piece of dung. That's pretty much how I grew to view so much of the news media after having so many negative experiences with them. I wouldn't even hazard a guess as to how many positive stories of accomplishment and achievement in my school district never found their way into print during my fifteen years as Upper Darby's superintendent of schools. But it was far too many.

And then there was selective editing. If ten topics were addressed at a school board meeting, how could only three or four of these issues typically get newspaper coverage from the reporters who were there and eventually wrote stories? Yet that's what regularly happened. The public's right to know, allegedly so sacred in newsrooms, really meant the public's right to know what editors and writers had decided to tell them.

Anything negative about the school system usually got automatic, prominent coverage. Sometimes, the sources were highly questionable. Sometimes, the arguments or complaints were absurd. And often, some relatively insignificant incident that was given a sensationalized, overblown limelight by one citizen, gained front page coverage in a news article. In-depth coverage of any issue almost always gave way to the simplistic and the superficial. Statistical insights of these news media geniuses were totally lacking. You had to wonder how some of these people ever got through college.

CHAPTER 23

What I experienced too many times during my fifteen-year career as a school superintendent was the very worst of shoddy journalism. News stories with insufficient research, absurd analogies, biased perspectives, secondary rather than prime sources, witch hunts, and an exaggerated "beat the dead horse" emphasis on the negative from reporters and editors were typical, not unusual, during my tenure. Not exactly journalism's finest hour.

Small wonder that the public really doesn't think too much of the fourth estate. A Report Card on the Press resulting from a Pew Research Center for the People and the Press survey (reported in *USA Today*, April 23, 1999) has revealed that *38 percent of the American people think that the press is immoral* and *67 percent believe that the news media has no regard for the people they report on*. Gee, from my perspective, these figures are much too generous.

At this point, I would be remiss if I didn't point out that the public school establishment has to share part of the blame for news media travesties. Too many school administrators simply do not fight back when their teachers or their schools are abused. Many consciously choose to protect their careers by staying away from the spotlight. Some are just plain cowardly. Still others are too stupid to realize the damaging impacts of inaccuracies and falsehoods being spread to the public at large. School administrators need to fight back much more than they're doing at present. There's no room for cowardice here.

24

IS A MIRACLE
NEWSWORTHY?

Proud of his Japanese heritage, Johnny had excelled academically at Upper Darby High School. He went on to Temple University with everything going for him. Then, one day, he was just in the wrong place at the wrong time. At a subway station in Philadelphia, he was shot in the head in an attempted robbery.

Miraculously, John recovered from the doorstep of death. Amazingly, he was graduated magna cum laude from Temple in 1995. In an emotional address at Temple's commencement, this pre-med student spoke before Bill Cosby and six thousand fellow graduates and their families and stole the show.

Partly, it was because John was the first commencement speaker in Temple University history to give part of his speech in Japanese. But, more importantly, in his eight-minute speech, he told of his struggle to overcome adversity. He challenged his audience to make a better world through the "extraordinarily simple act of caring." Caring was something that John said he learned in the Upper Darby School District.

With all that John had overcome, it was truly his day to shine. But he chose instead to dwell poignantly and dramatically on his many positive experiences in the Upper Darby School District.

I still lift myself up today with thoughts of John, who, by the way, is currently a practicing physician. It's the stuff that makes us public educators tick and keep on ticking. Just one of my pocket full of miracles. And, unfortunately, it's the kind of terrific story the news media all too often ignore. In America these days, it's too much of the wrong stuff that gets all the play. Our nation deserves better.

25

THE MAD BOMBER

To whom this may concern,

I, Robert Landoff will follow Timothy Mcviegh's footsteps on December 6, 1995, & blow up the DHMS middle school in PA. I won't be arriving in any big truck full of explosives. I won't even be there at the time of the S. boom. I hope you will evacuate the children from the building. If you don't it will be your own stupid fault. This is all I will say about this.
  BANG, BANG, BANG, BANG, BANG, BANG, BANG.
  Ha, HA, Ha, HA, Ha, HA, Ha............!!!!!

                                                            y, By, By, By

On Saturday afternoon, November 18, 1995, a conscientious security guard at an area hospital, more than ten miles from the Upper Darby School District, discovered a note in a hospital corridor. It threatened to explode the Drexel Hill Middle School in Upper Darby on a specific date. It was neatly folded and lying on the floor. It had been created on what appeared to be a manual typewriter. The guard speculated someone had accidentally dropped it. He wasn't at all sure what to make of it. He gave the note to a supervisor who called the Pennsylvania State Police, who then funneled the information to the Upper Darby police.

I met with representatives of the Upper Darby and state police on Sunday morning. They were as pale as ghosts. The bombing of the Oklahoma City federal facility was too vivid and too recent. I asked them to evaluate the credibility of the note. They refused to speculate. They had no idea. I demanded that they involve the FBI.

On Monday evening, two days after the bomb threat was found, my school board and I met in emergency session with two local FBI agents and Upper Darby's police leaders. Interestingly enough, the township's elected officials declined an invitation to attend the meeting even though by now they were aware of the subject matter. Not their problem! Politics at its worst—the school district left out on a limb.

I kept pressing law enforcement authorities for an evaluation of the threat. Was it real or not? Give me some accurate odds. What the hell did any of us in the school system know about mad bombers? Finally, one of the FBI clones went out on the limb and said that there was a fifty-fifty chance the threat was real. Gee, what a big help. Then, one of these J. Edgar Hoover types informed our group that the FBI would only be providing supplemental assistance in this matter since the Upper Darby police were the lead investigating agency. A matter of government policy. Then why do we need an FBI? What the hell did the Upper Darby cops know about mad bombers? We were all out of our league here and being left on our own.

The next evening, the school board held another special meeting behind closed doors. One of my board members, a corporate attorney, had Washington, D.C., clients who did security work at the White House and other governmental facilities. He arranged for two of the "spooks" to provide us with some gratis help.

The security firm representatives had visited the Drexel Hill Middle School facility earlier that afternoon. They were horrified. Lots of entrances and exits. No metal detectors. Teachers and students going in and out throughout the day. Delivery people and parents and other visitors coming and going at will. Recreational activities by community groups every evening. What the hell did they expect? This was a public school, not some dictator's heavily guarded headquarters. They thought the note might be the real thing. They indicated that there was a chance the bomb was already planted.

We spent a long evening developing a game plan. No public disclosure for another week. Try to keep all this under wraps for as long as possible so as to not compromise the police investigation. If we didn't catch the villain by next Monday, December 4, two days before the threatened explosion, we would have to go public. Don't panic the community until it's absolutely necessary.

We arranged with the Philadelphia police to engage their bomb sniffing dogs. It's interesting that no such service exists among law enforcement in the entire Delaware County. Oh, and forget any ideas of neighborly courtesy from Philly. We were going to pay through the nose for the use of the dogs. The week before the bomb was scheduled to explode we had three confidential midnight sweeps of the school building. All came up empty. But we were told that the dogs have trouble picking up plastic explosives. A great vote of confidence.

The cops and my computer people scanned thousands of school district employee and parent names for a connection to Robert Landoff, the name in the bomb note. We gained access to tons of records at the area hospital where it all started. We had people working twenty-four hours around the clock looking for some connection in names of hospital employees and patients. At the Drexel Hill Middle School, we focused on suspensions and parent complaints for the past three years. Since no student in the school district had the name, Robert Landoff, we checked for step parents and recent divorces, a maddening task. Not a clue. I went to bed every night, but didn't sleep.

On Monday, December 4, we went public. I told the faculty at Drexel Hill Middle School everything first thing in the morning. Unless a miracle happened, we would be closed on Wednesday, the "day of the bomb." Most people handled it well, but not all. Lots of blank stares of disbelief. Fear and terror written on many faces. Some tears. The school administrators would tell the students that afternoon right before dismissal. Each pupil would take home an explanatory letter to parents.

I headed back to work for a scheduled press conference, something rarely done in the school district. I laid the debacle on the reporters. They loved it. The next morning, all the newspapers had front page accounts of the intended bombing. In response, we probably fielded a thousand calls between the school and the administration building. The epidemic spread. Parents of students even at our other schools wanted to know if their kids were safe. Some people kept their children home from school.

In terms of television and newspaper coverage, this event blew the top off the Richter Scale. But that was the only explosion. There was no bomb. The school sat ominously quiet surrounded by police security and television trucks from midnight through the next twenty-four hours on Wednesday, December 6. Nothing happened. Absolutely nothing. The next morning, we nervously reopened the school.

Later that same day, an eighth grader at Drexel Hill Middle School, accompanied by his priest and his mother, turned himself in to the Upper Darby police. He confessed to the crime. It never became clear as to why the student authored such a note, but he told police he never intended for anyone to see it. He *claimed* that he dropped it by accident. The priest pleaded the case. The cops bought in to his innocence. No charges would be filed. The county district attorney backed away as well. All was forgiven.

Except by me. I issued the following public statement:

> I am very concerned that the consequences for the thirteen-year-old juvenile who has admitted authoring the savage threat against the Drexel Hill Middle School have been eliminated by our legal system. Clearly, that system is broken!
>
> It has sadly become an all too common reality throughout American society that those who have hurt others use the tired cliché of "I didn't mean it or I never intended to do it." I do not and will not accept such a rationalization.
>
> Let there be no mistake here. Our school community has been a victim. We have squandered taxpayer dollars trying to prevent a disaster. We have wasted the energies of our police department and many school system employees. We have teachers who have needed psychological help in response to this act. We have reports of students still experiencing nightmares. Families of our students have had to deal with fear brought into their homes from school. This is totally unacceptable.
>
> No explanation or expression of remorse can excuse what happened here.
>
> If we are to maintain a civilized society, there must be severe penalties for this perpetrator. If not, we are endorsing anarchy and chaos.

I received a great deal of mail as well as a ton of phone calls after my statement was published. The overwhelming majority was supportive, mostly from parents and teachers. A few liberal community residents thought I was too harsh. And columnists from two different newspapers ripped me for being too tough. Are these the same people who regularly write about a lack of discipline in public schools?

My God, this kid shouted *fire* in a crowded theater, and all hell broke loose. According to the perp, he didn't want to cause any trouble. And now we were all supposed to roll over for this behavior. Not in my school district. We moved to expel the student. In finest American tradition, the mother obtained a lawyer. The shill demanded that the school district back off. I never blinked or thought about blinking. The student transferred into a private school. The matter ended.

26

HAIL TO THE CHIEF

Late in the afternoon of October 4, 1988, I received a call from the powerful Republican leader of Upper Darby. Big John rarely bothered me. I knew this was something important. He informed me that President Ronald Reagan would be visiting Upper Darby High in eight days, on Wednesday, October 12. A group of "front people" from the White House as well as Secret Service agents would be arriving tomorrow to meet with the appropriate administrators to arrange everything.

We picked up the delegation the next morning in private cars. They landed in a United States of America jet on an isolated runway behind a secluded Philadelphia airport terminal I never knew existed. We whisked them to an Upper Darby restaurant some twenty minutes away for our meeting.

This was a very interesting group. The president's Washington bodyguards, two Marine helicopter pilots, a U.S. Navy captain of some sort, a host of Secret Service agents from the Philadelphia office, a dozen or so political operatives, two speech writers, two appointment executives, the White House chief of staff, and the press secretary.

There wasn't much give and take. These people were used to giving orders. And I suppose even I could be subservient to get my kids a chance to see the president of the United States.

The Upper Darby High School event would last twenty minutes. We could have only juniors and seniors present. That's because we were mandated to invite an equal number of students from the two Catholic high schools down the street. A good dose of the politically correct. A beaming

Reagan, in the twilight of his presidency, surrounded by adoring students. That was the image the White House was looking for next Wednesday.

But back to the president at Upper Darby High and the week of preparations to get ready. The Secret Service decided on a dirty, smelly coaches' locker room area in the school basement as the "staging area" for the president. This was where he would "catch his breath" after arriving and before addressing the students.

Maybe this was a good choice for security reasons, but the place was a pig sty. Our maintenance crews went to work. Within forty-eight hours, the place was fumigated, freshly painted, and new and brighter lighting was installed. One of my school board members was a furniture retailer. He supplied a sofa, arm chair, lamps, end tables, and rugs. The place became a very nice apartment.

The library was chosen as the press room. More than two hundred news media types would soon be utilizing this facility. The Secret Service chose the high school's nonglittery gymnasium for the president's speech. Why they rejected the much more attractive and larger school auditorium remains a mystery. But you can bet it had something to do with the gym being a safer alternative.

White House personnel showed up a few days before the happening and constructed the podium area with bulletproof glass and other impenetrable materials. The gymnasium was then sealed off from all use forty-eight hours prior to the visit. Secret Service agents were all over the place during those two days.

Finally, the Upper Darby High School band had to learn a special arrangement of "Hail to the Chief." We already had the music, but for some reason it was unacceptable. All was in readiness.

The actual presidential visit was nothing short of spectacular for our school community. October 12, 1988. Thousands of people lined the streets and waved as the president's motorcade sped through Upper Darby. The gymnasium was wonderfully disguised with red, white, and blue artwork and streamers everywhere. The enthusiasm of several thousand high school students lit up the atmosphere.

The content of President Reagan's speech was disappointing. Too much politics and Republican propaganda. Vouchers, bring back prayer to the schools, and elect George Bush! But Reagan's unique personal charisma carried the day as it so often did. The guy was magical. This presidential happening was absolutely electric! Cynic that I am, even I was impressed by Reagan's aura.

Now let's have just a bit of reality therapy before we all faint with ecstasy.

As a *candidate* for president in 1980, Reagan had given a fiery speech in Upper Darby High's auditorium. That night, he was in his prime and he was at his best, stirring and moving a partisan Republican crowd. Now he had come back to where he started. A meaningful symbolic gesture! But it was eight years later, and his prowess was fading away. Time eventually ravages all of us. He was no longer a spring chicken. The Iran-Contra scandal had also taken its toll. This once glib president was very much restricted to prepared text by his advisors. Ad-libbing was now severely curtailed. And Reagan was surrounded and guarded not so much by bodyguards, but by people making sure he didn't say the wrong thing.

When Reagan arrived at Upper Darby High, his contingent immediately hustled him downstairs to the living room area, which had been transformed from the coaches' locker room.

I was among a small group of school district VIPs lingering near the president. He kept repeating to those around him that he had no idea that high schools had these pretty apartments in their basements. This was all very nice, but what exactly do they use it for? Does somebody live here? An aide literally dragged Reagan away toward his private bathroom. That'll be enough of that.

On our way up to the gymnasium, I grabbed for a moment in the sun with the president. I asked if he approved of the attacks being perpetrated on public schools by William Bennett, who had used the Office of Secretary of Education as a bully pulpit for ripping public education. Reagan responded that he couldn't understand this, because he *liked public schools and didn't know who this Bennett fellow was.* A presidential staffer's eyes burned laser holes deeply into my body. She pulled the president out of my reach. I didn't have any more questions, anyway. "Was it possible the president didn't know who William Bennett was?"

These were just a couple of clues. What happened a few minutes later is more telling. Reagan had just finished his speech. The crowd was on its feet applauding. Our student leaders had wanted to give the president an Upper Darby High School sweatshirt and a football pennant. However, they were mandated to give the president an over-sized report card with an A+. The White House advisors had come up with this report card, and it worked terrifically well with the press. If they had asked me, I would have given the President a D— for the anti–public education propaganda his administration had dished out over the past eight years. Anyway, the crowd loved the whole thing. More cheering.

Reagan raised his arms to quiet the audience. He was trying to do an ad-lib commentary. This was not permitted. Crisis among the White House advisors.

Directly beneath the president's podium was the Upper Darby High School band. They were surrounded by lots of event people with earphones who were connected to the White House orchestrators in a central viewing area. The script called for playing the "Stars and Stripes Forever."

But the president wanted to speak. A panicked voice exclaimed to all of the earphones: "Start the music, now!" The crowd was now quiet. Reagan opened his mouth to speak. This time the voice in the earphones screamed out frantically: "Start that damn music immediately. That's an order!"

Within a split second, the "Stars and Stripes Forever" drowned out the president of the United States. Reagan relaxed and gave up trying to speak. He waved and smiled. I guess he was getting used to this.

As an epitaph, you may wonder what happened to the apartment in the high school basement. Well, first of all, after the president had long departed from the high school, a group of school board members and locally elected officials revisited the "living room." Some wanted to sit on the furniture where Reagan sat. Some wanted to use the toilet that he used. True worshippers.

The apartment was eventually disassembled, and its furniture returned to the school board member who had loaned it to us. He put it in his showroom and sold it quickly for a nice profit. President or no president, our coaches were glad to have their locker room finally returned to them. And they even got a needed paint job out of the deal!

27

SOME THOUGHTS
ON MY LEADERSHIP

Someone once theorized that great leaders are usually surrounded by great people. In my case, this was absolutely true. I inherited a staff of principals and central administrators who were young, bright, and willing. What a leader should bring to his or her people is focus and direction. And that's what I did. No administrator who ever worked for me was ever unsure about where I was coming from.

From my very first administrative staff meeting, the priorities were set:

We are all about kids; If necessary, we will fight on their behalf!
We will constantly seek to innovate and get better.
We will compete! And,
When we succeed, we will tell people about it!

Over the years, I gave administrators and school faculties "plenty of rope." The biggest mistake that school superintendents make is trying to micromanage the activities of others. That practice only wastes the talents, ingenuity, and leadership of others.

So what happened while I was at the helm? The answer is, *plenty!* But I didn't do anything alone! I unified and supported the efforts of others. Together, we prioritized our beliefs about schools and children. In that context, we implemented all sorts of change. We held our programs up for external evaluation in all sorts of competitions. We took risks. And we experienced success beyond our wildest dreams.

CHAPTER 27

Through it all, I defined, demanded, inspired, motivated, reinforced, and complimented. And then, I got the hell out of the way. That's what leadership is all about. Many Upper Darby School District people rose up. The school system soared:

- Six of the district's twelve schools earned the prestigious "Blue Ribbon" National Award of Excellence.
- The first Teacher Center in eastern Pennsylvania was opened in the Upper Darby School District. Dedicated to the improvement and enhancement of teaching, the center retrained hundreds of Upper Darby's own teachers as well as numerous staff members from Greater Philadelphia's public and parochial schools.
- The school district attained national recognition for its large School-Business Network of Partnerships and its Arts Education programs.
- The school system's Drug Prevention Initiatives and Parent Involvement Network were recognized as exemplary by the Commonwealth of Pennsylvania.
- A Performing Arts Center was established to exponentially expand cultural and theatrical opportunities for the community.
- A program of privately endowed scholarships and mentoring, modeled on the Philadelphia Futures Project, was set up at Upper Darby High School. It is the largest of its kind in Greater Philadelphia suburbia.
- A cyclical, ongoing review process was established to keep all curricula current and state of the art; unified discipline codes were put in place at all levels of the school system.
- The school district received six consecutive clean audits of its finances and professional certification records (covering twelve years) from the state of Pennsylvania.
- The school system amicably settled fifteen consecutive contract agreements with its three unions.
- Unique partnerships to benefit students were implemented with Philadelphia's Channel 10 (NBC affiliate) and with Boeing Helicopters.
- A "model" centralized Kindergarten Center was established to improve early childhood learning for Upper Darby's diverse pupil population.

- To accommodate the school system's rapid growth, two formerly closed schools were brought back from the dead, and four other schools were renovated and enlarged. All of this was accomplished under budget and on remarkably tight schedule timelines.

Finally, I should tell you that when I've lectured to graduate students in educational administration at various universities, they have invariably asked me how I survived for fifteen years in one school district. This could have been a reference to the average career life of a suburban school superintendent being about five years, and an urban superintendent about two years. But it was not. In my case, these graduate students were trying to understand how the very high profile, very public, and often very controversial Upper Darby School District superintendent could have lasted so long.

What I've always told these graduate students is that being a school superintendent should never be about survival. Unfortunately, too many of my colleagues were obsessed with that. They practiced being invisible. And it was wrong! Being a superintendent of schools should first and foremost be about moral high ground. It's all a matter of deciding whether or not some issue is relevant enough to fight for and die for. You can't make decisions about something as important as students and schools in a context of personal consequences. You just do the right thing!

28

MUSIC . . . THE EGALITARIAN COMPONENT

For many students across America, what they're asked to study in school is frequently artificial and meaningless to them. That's because what's real is outside the school in the world in which they're trying to survive. Well-intentioned teachers are often trying to impart content or encourage interest in areas that have zero relevance to many of their students. Many pupils from nonprivileged backgrounds need some relevancy hook to get them into the world of academia. I should know. I was one of them!

Early in my career as Upper Darby's superintendent of schools, I was searching for some lever to create more relevance, self-esteem and unity among my very heterogeneous student body at all levels. I found the answer in music education, and the greatest music faculty ever assembled in one school district.

The goal was simple. Make it egalitarian, attractive to the masses. Get as many students as possible involved in music, but don't sacrifice any quality. To make this happen, I tapped a visionary leader from our ranks. Barbara was a new music supervisor and was undaunted by the task. She built a monster of music excellence that encompassed every school in the district. I kept challenging her to get better. She kept pushing the music faculty to go on to the next level. The whole thing was awesome.

During his campaign for president, Robert Kennedy once said, "Some people see things as they are and ask *why,* but I see things as they might be, and say *why not!*" That must have been the motto for Upper Darby's music teachers.

CHAPTER 28

Our performing groups were first rate and won many competitions. Our Senior High Marching Band was an invited "regular" at the Miss America Pageant Parade in Atlantic City. And our Concert Choir performed on numerous occasions with the Philadelphia Orchestra. But that is not what egalitarianism is about. What was so much more impressive and significant is that the Upper Darby High Winter Concert at Christmas annually featured more than 400 student performers. No other Greater Philadelphia High School was putting that number of kids on the stage for their moment in the sun. At the same time, elementary and middle school concerts across the school district followed suit. Large numbers of pupils were engaged in creative, wondrous concerts. I know because I attended most of them.

Egalitarian madness is what we were after. In 1997, we actually held an all-school concert that featured more than one thousand pupils in our Performing Arts Center. Just imagine the logistics of getting one thousand students to one place, yet alone having them know what to do and when to do it! Kids of all sizes and all ages and with a wide range of talent in an absolutely spectacular performance. My best dream come true, and one of my fondest memories.

And finally, I should mention Veteran's Stadium in Philadelphia. In 1999, led by Brad, another of my music teacher maniacs, we think that we set a new world record with an eight-hundred-piece school district marching mega band prior to a Phillies game. There are no words for this one. You had to be there to see it to believe it!

In summary, music was one means to offer every Upper Darby student something without any artificiality, something that was very real, enjoyable, and pursuable in later life. Whether students had disabilities, family problems, academic prowess, or limited English proficiency didn't matter. Over the years, thousands and thousands of Upper Darby kids mingled together in music spectaculars regardless of their abilities or backgrounds. For many of them, music gave meaning and relevance to school, and led them into other things like literature, science, and mathematics. For me, this was a source of great joy and fulfillment. My secret weapon—an egalitarian educational monstrosity! *The way it's supposed to be!*

29

THE JAPANESE
VISITORS

During my fifteen years as a school superintendent, our school district hosted a number of visiting delegations from across America and around the world. We had had previous visitors from Japan in 1990, but they were simply tourists who had paid some exorbitant price for an educational tour.

In 1994, the entourage of Japanese educators that arrived in our district was sent by their government through an arrangement with our Department of State. They were strictly business, working intensely through the three days, taking tons of notes and not smiling much.

The leader of the Japanese delegation was an older man, a principal of an elementary school back home. Through the group translator, he boomed out long spurts of very loud Japanese that sounded like *I hate your guts*. But the translation was often *what an interesting curriculum* or *what a lovely painting* on that wall. I asked the interpreter about this and she told me it was simply *his way. The old way of tradition.*

At the welcome breakfast for the Japanese educators, our principals and a number of school board members were in attendance. It was very stiff and formal. Through the translator, I inquired as to how many school districts were on their itinerary. His reply stunned all of us:

This delegation includes representative educators from every province of Japan. We have come to see only one school system. This one! It is the socioeconomic and ethnic diversity of your school system that we are studying.

CHAPTER 29

Japan must change. It must become more egalitarian in its educational system. Our recommendations to the Japanese Ministry of Education will be based on what we see here. The reputation of this school system is well known in Japan. That is why we are here.

So here's a nation from thousands of miles away giving my school district the respect it so richly deserved. While in our own backyard, like many public school systems, we struggled on a daily basis for dignity and self-esteem from the outside. Remarkably ironic.

The Japanese visitors were not disappointed in what they saw. The richness of curriculum choices astonished them. The quality of teaching impressed them. They were incredulous that we mainstreamed special education children into regular classrooms. They couldn't believe that the vast majority of our emotionally disturbed children and mentally retarded pupils were not farmed out to special schools. The ethnic diversity fascinated them; young people who were mortal enemies in other lands walked arm-in-arm through our corridors. And finally, the Japanese visitors were overwhelmed by the kindness, friendliness, and hospitality of our students and teachers. Welcome to America's failing public schools.

As a culminating event and an expression of gratitude, the Japanese delegation invited my school board and all the district administrators to dine with them at their headquarters in the Sheraton Society Hill Hotel in center city Philadelphia. I expected protocol and formality. I was wrong.

The Japanese visitors were clad in kimonos. There was an open bar. Everyone was soon very happy.

I was finishing my third martini when the leader of the delegation, now my good friend, invited me to take center stage with him. He gave a wonderfully gracious thank you speech for, as he put it, our sharing the essence of our being as educators with them.

He and I drank plum wine from a ceremonial friendship bowl that was then passed around for every person in the room to also have a taste. I still have that bowl. A cherished possession.

The Japanese leader then ordered his group to assemble and they sang *three* songs to us in their native language. I wasn't going to be outdone. I ordered the school board, all nine of them, as well as my administrators, to gather together. We dedicated the *four* songs we sang in English to our guests. Everyone was very moved. The bar was still open. We drank some more.

Thank goodness, dinner was finally served. A wonderful feast accompanied by saki and champagne. The room got noisy. Lots of laughter and good cheer. By evening's end, the entire Upper Darby School District contingent had on kimonos and matching headband scarves given to us by our visitors. We reciprocated, making presents for our Japanese colleagues out of our ties, coats, hats, pens, and whatever else we could get our hands on. Everyone was sorry to see the evening end. Many of us were tearful as we said sayonara.

I had driven into Philly with my assistant, Bernie, in his meticulous Cadillac. We had valet parked it. Bernie and I looked like the poor man's imitation of samurai as we left the hotel and headed to the parking lot. But we decided that to remove our kimonos and headbands would be an insult to our Japanese gift-givers. So we kept them on. The faces of the valet attendants said it all. So they thought we were whackos. What did we care? Tonight we were Japanese and proud of it.

The ride back from Philly was almost uneventful. But then we had to stop for a red light at 52nd and Walnut, a notorious intersection. Four drug pushers were on the corner peering into our car.

"Look at them (deleted expletives) in that Caddy," one of our admirers exclaimed. "What in the (deleted expletive) do you think they be?"

I was on the passenger's side closest to them. I yelled out the window. "Haven't you dumb junkies ever seen real Japanese people? You've been usin' too much of the stuff you sell. You and your goddamned drugs can go to hell!"

The pushers gave us one finger salutes. A terrified Bernie burned rubber out of there, and we sped away toward Upper Darby, only minutes away. I often wonder how we would have handled the explanation if the cops had pulled over the Upper Darby School District's two top administrators so strangely attired. Thank God, we didn't find out that night.

30

GOD, HOW
I HATE SNOW!

I have often been asked what was the worst part of being a school superintendent? For me, that answer was always an easy one. Snow days. The previous superintendent, Mike, always said the same thing, but when I was a young, naive assistant superintendent I couldn't understand his point. What could be so tough? Just make the call!

Well, you've got to walk the walk to know what this is all about. It's a very lonely experience. And it's terrifying. Most of the time, you experience this horror in the darkness of the early morning, when you're trying to figure out whether or not to open schools. Nothing much to worry about here. Just the safety of thousands of students that depends on your crystal ball. You think about a few school busses crashing on your watch and a horde of kids admitted to area hospitals. These are not pleasant thoughts!

No conscientious superintendent has ever slept much on these nights. Usually, you're an insomniac, awake, shivering, prowling the house, and periodically peering outside. None of this does any good. That's the recurring nightmare. Colleagues telephone you. They say they don't know what to do. You reply that you don't know what to do either. You stare fear in the face. *Close the schools. Open the schools. Delay opening the schools. Who the hell knows? Just don't let anyone get hurt!*

Through the night, weather forecasters are right there with you on radio and television predicting the end of the world with the approaching snowstorm. And, of course, most of them are generally clueless. *Well, it could be two inches of snow, but if this or that happens, we could get ten inches. Well, it might change to rain, but if this or that happens, it could become an ice storm and turn everything into an ice skating rink. Of course, it could just pass us by and we'll get nothing.*

My least favorite people in the world. Meteorologists. Advanced science degrees, satellites, radar, all kinds of electronics. Totally useless!

Once you've handled snow and ice storms a few times, you learn that (1) the news media has one simple goal when inclement weather approaches—to scare everyone to death! So it's better to ignore whatever they're saying. (2) The vast majority of weather forecasters do not come close to predicting what eventually happens. Pay no attention to these people. (3) Rational decision-making about inclement weather is an impossibility. Follow what your gut tells you and most of the time you'll be okay. And (4) no matter what you decide to do, it's very probable that half your constituents will say you were wrong. So get used to being called an idiot!

And so, I present you with the chart below. It's scientifically based on my dealings with more than seventy snow and ice storms during my career as a school superintendent. Use it well!

Most Effective Ways To Predict Weather
(Ranked from Most Accurate to Least Accurate)

Most Accurate   1. Ask Your Local Fortune Teller
                             2. Check Your Horoscope
                             3. Roll the Dice
                             4. Get Your Palm Read
                             5. Visit Your Local Witch
                             6. Voodoo
                             7. How Does Your Bunion Feel?
                             8. Look Out the Window
                             9. The National Weather Service
Least Accurate   10. Television and Radio Weather Persons

31

THE FIRE OF '93

On New Year's Day afternoon, Friday, January 1, 1993, Joan and I were sipping champagne and watching the Philadelphia Mummer's Parade on television. The phone call came from the Upper Darby police. One of my schools was burning. I grabbed my parka and ran out the door.

When I arrived at the Bywood School just five minutes from my home, things were chaotic. Fire engines all over. The smell of smoke. Lots of broken windows. Water all over the schoolyard. I nearly vomited.

Bywood was one of my larger elementary schools. Lots of immigrant newcomers and poor children went to school here. We had no other available space. What the hell was I going to do?

Thank heavens, the fire had been quickly extinguished. But this looked like big trouble. The fire marshall accompanied me inside. There was smoke and water damage everywhere. At the origin of the fire, the two malfunctioning boilers that supplied the heat for the building were totally disabled. It was the middle of a cold winter. At first glance, it appeared that Bywood would be closed indefinitely for many weeks, perhaps months. My heart was in my mouth.

For those of you who are not that astute, I should explain that you can't go out over the weekend and pick up a replacement commercial boiler. Of course, we ordered a new one immediately. But it had to be shipped from Kansas and would take two weeks at the minimum for delivery. My maintenance supervisor, Mike, the eternal optimist, kept telling me not to worry. He said he was already making some calls. He told me to get some sleep and come back in the morning. Things would be better. I thought he was dreaming.

I staggered down to the school basement. I joined the cleaning crews trying to get rid of soot, oil, and water simultaneously. I didn't accomplish much. But the therapy was wonderful. I had to feel like I was doing something. And there was solid camaraderie being with my workers. I went home dirty and beaten at 4:00 A.M.

When I returned to the Bywood School early the next morning, Saturday, January 2, no less than forty cars were parked in the school yard. Every one of my maintenance staff had come on site to take on the problem. This was supposed to have been a well-deserved long weekend for them with their families. There were also five different heating contractors on the scene. The place was a beehive. What we really needed was divine intervention!

Heroic round-the-clock effort created a miracle. The smoke and water damage was cleaned up with forty-eight non-stop hours of elbow grease. It was dirty, nasty work. One boiler was miraculously retrofitted and reactivated within seventy-two hours. Don't ask me what kept it running. Paper clips, band aids, rubber bands? We gained enough marginal heat to keep the Bywood School open until the new boilers arrived. We lost one school day at Bywood. In any other normal school district, a school in that situation would have been closed for months.

Maybe it was because my father was a maintenance guy. I don't know. But I think it was because of the maximum performance they always gave me. I loved my maintenance staff.

Bywood's eight hundred students had lost their school to a fire on January 1, 1993. Four days later, my miracle workers had put it back into working order. When the crisis passed and the new heating system was alive and well at Bywood, I brought every single maintenance person to a meeting and honored them before the school board. That was in public. Privately, each got a different reward. I purchased a bottle of good champagne for each and every one of them. But there was nothing I could have done to express adequate appreciation for this massive accomplishment.

Through a hundred other facility crises during my fifteen years, my maintenance people were always there by my side. And never ever once did they fail me.

32

MOM TAKES CHARGE!

Upper Darby High School football fortunes rose up from the ashes while I was superintendent of schools. My high school principal, Gil, and I drank many martinis after many losses when we first got our jobs. We didn't like losing. We fixed the problem with the help of a corps of determined disciples including Jack, a charismatic, come-follow-me coach. Upper Darby became a winner on the gridiron. It didn't happen overnight, but it happened!

When I came to the school district, the community buzz was that we would never beat Monsignor Bonner, the Catholic high school down the street from Upper Darby High, because Catholic schools had discipline and public schools didn't. After Upper Darby defeated Monsignor Bonner for the sixth time in seven years, there's no more talk in the community about which school has more discipline.

In 1988, we had a senior lineman who was clearly a Division I prospect. Todd was around 260 pounds, strong and fast. The recruiters showed up en masse, including Notre Dame's Lou Holtz.

Holtz flew Todd out to South Bend for a weekend, where he stayed in the coach's home and was fed delicious fare by Mrs. Holtz. This was all the potential dream come true for this very Catholic student athlete. When he returned to Upper Darby, Todd had "Fighting Irish" stars in his eyes. He had seen the Golden Dome and many ghosts of past Notre Dame football greats. It was all over but the signing.

Two days later, Penn State's legendary Joe Paterno showed up at our school for his recruiting visit with Todd. At Paterno's request, Todd's mom was present. They met in a tiny closet-like room at the high school. Paterno's pitch was remarkably simple. He addressed it to mom, not Todd. *If he comes to Penn State, the most important thing is that he's gonna graduate with a degree on schedule. How do I know this? Because if he starts to screw around academically, I'll smack him in the side of the head! He'll also play football, but that comes second!*

Now I'm sure that Notre Dame is a very good academic institution, and that Lou Holtz is a very fine man. But this ball game was over for the Fighting Irish. Paterno hit the parent bull's-eye. Mom was in charge here. Parenting at its very best!

Maybe he would have done just as well at Notre Dame, but Todd became a Penn State football player that day. He eventually had a great career as an offensive lineman for the Nittany Lions, and of course was graduated on time. Later, he went on to become a starter for the NFL's New England Patriots. And most importantly, he never forgot where he came from. To this day, Todd regularly returns to the schools he attended to motivate and inspire Upper Darby kids.

I've loved telling this anecdote on the speech circuit. I've used it a hundred times as a lead-in to the point that parents make the difference in the education of their children more than anything else. As a superintendent of schools I have firsthand knowledge of thousands of student success stories in our schools, and the consistent thread running through each of these cases has been strong backing from the home. From infancy through age eighteen, children spend approximately 92 percent of their time outside the school walls and under the direct influence of parents. And that is where the real action has been and continues to be. Certainly, public schools need to constantly improve and find newer and better ways to do what they do. But that is only a part of the educational success equation. Strong parenting matters even more!

33

THE POWER
OF WHITEFISH

I've always had great admiration for teacher unions. It was a long battle for them over many years. But today they have managed to bring dignity and decent wages to a profession that was previously underrated and grossly underpaid in America.

If you take a hard look at the most vociferous critics of unions in America these days, usually you'll find corporate types with vested interests (no sense in sharing too much profit with the workers), and also, some just plain ol' wealthy folks who will never have enough money.

My wife, Joan, had this illogical acquaintance from a very affluent community who was always chirping about high teacher salaries. This woman actually went to a school board meeting to protest the fact that a thirty-year veteran teacher could make $75,000. Of course, you couldn't afford a home in this community unless your salary exceeded $150,000. And her husband, an oil company executive, was pulling down more than $200,000 per annum.

In 1966, my second year as a teacher, I told Joan's dad that I wanted to marry his daughter. Her father, a union millwright, had great reservations. He liked me well enough, but as a teacher, I had no financial future. How could I support his daughter? At the time, he was right. He gave me a bunch of electronics magazines. *Read these and get a new career*. I politely accepted them and threw them in the trash. The next year I married Joan. We struggled financially during those years. *But we were the teachers we both wanted to be. We were also a perfect illustration of why teacher union militancy was needed!*

CHAPTER 33

In the Upper Darby School District, there were two nasty teacher strikes during the 1970s. Management and labor relations were very strained. In 1980, Mike became the superintendent of schools. And he elevated me to an assistant superintendent position that included the personnel arena.

Mike was very shrewd. For the monthly required meet and discuss sessions with teacher union leaders, he was somehow able to persuade them to utilize Drexelbrook, a very plush local restaurant facility with private rooms and bar service. We met in the late afternoons after school was dismissed. The union leaders and Mike engaged in a 4:30 P.M. cocktail hour ritual. The only one who didn't drink was me. Mike forbade it, because someone had to stay completely sober and record whatever happened. Usually, what did ensue after a few rounds of drinks was a great deal of stalemating on union concerns and issues. Some settlement of critical problems of course did occasionally occur, but for the most part, this delaying action each month miraculously kept the two sides away from the hostilities of the past.

Like a good pupil, I marveled that Mike was able to get away with this. When he retired in 1984, I had no intention of changing his very successful labor relations strategy. And then along came Rene. She was the very sharp, good-looking new president of Upper Darby's teachers' union. I looked forward to the monthly drinking rituals with such a pretty woman, because now I could join the imbibers while my new assistant, Bernie, would have to take the notes. Union relations might not be so bad!

Unfortunately, Rene was too idealistic. One of those change agents! *Drexelbrook was over,* she dictated. She wanted to meet in the early morning hours before school. We were going to solve a million teacher union concerns together. I was devastated.

Rene asked me for my input on her idea. A rhetorical question! Her mind was clearly made up. No sense arguing with a hard-headed woman. But I decided to get something.

"I want *whitefish*. It's the only way I'll do this!" I defiantly told Rene. She had no idea what I was talking about. I went for the gold. "Whitefish and bagels are what I'd rather eat for breakfast than anything else. I'll meet in the morning, but only if the union supplies the best whitefish you can find every month." Rene smiled her beautiful smile. We cut the deal. My prowess as a negotiator was never more evident!

Over the next fifteen years, I shared whitefish with seven different teacher union presidents on more than one hundred mornings. At times, we fought with each other. But mostly, we compromised, listened to one another, and worked out some very complicated and/or emotional situations.

The fact of the matter is that too many of my colleague superintendents are constantly obsessing about their battles with the evil teacher unions. They should try whitefish. Right before I retired, all of the teacher union presidents with whom I dealt in my career hosted a special breakfast for me at which we celebrated the many years of wonderfully amicable management/union relationships. We all ate whitefish and bagels, and laughed a lot together! School administrators are not likely to admit this, but relationships with teacher unions are as good or as bad as the superintendent makes them.

34

THE CARDINAL PLAYS POLITICAL HARDBALL

The huge Archdiocesan School System that serves Greater Philadelphia has a proud history of success. Unfortunately, in recent years, its supply of free labor—priests, nuns, and brothers—has dried up. Religious vocations just aren't there to the extent they once were. Lay teachers cost money. And tuitions paid by parents of Catholic school pupils have been dramatically on the increase. And so, the Philadelphia Archdiocese had been "waging political war," in an attempt to get "voucher payments" to its parents to offset the costly tuition assessments for their children. I can almost sympathize with this effort. It actually makes some economic sense to keep these Catholic schools afloat. The public schools would have some real difficulty absorbing all of these students if the Greater Philadelphia parochial schools went under. So just tell it like it is!

However, the pitch line for this initiative has been questionable. Vouchers have been disguised by many politicians as an educational reform. But the reality in Pennsylvania, and specifically Greater Philadelphia, is that vouchers have been and continue to be about propping up the Catholic school system and not much else.

In early June of 1998, I was looking forward to a couple of weeks of summer vacation when all of a sudden, the Philadelphia Archdiocese boss, Anthony Cardinal Bevilacqua, decided to play some political hardball. The Archdiocese had lost a series of battles for their vouchers in Harrisburg in spite of strong support from its ally, Governor Ridge. So they decided to put the pressure on at the local level.

CHAPTER 34

Targeting school districts that had extensive numbers of Catholic schools in their community, the Cardinal suggested in a formal letter that those school systems, including mine, should just divert locally collected real estate tax money over to parents with children already in Catholic schools. The theory was that Catholic families with children in public schools would then transfer by the hundreds into the parochial schools since vouchers were available to them. And that would save dollars for the public schools!

Only in the Archdiocese dreams. Upper Darby families had been making philosophical choices about private, public, or parochial schools for their kids for many years. A $500 or even a $1000 bribe (voucher) wasn't going to change their convictions. And, of course, the most absurd part of the Cardinal's letter projected that, like Donald Trump, I could just head down to the vault and gather up a few million dollars that my school district had stored away and send it out to my Catholic school neighbors.

The astute Archdiocese press office had mailed the Cardinal's letter to the news media in advance. It set off a press feeding frenzy. Reporters were clamoring for a juicy response. Most of the "targeted" school system superintendents were shaking in their boots. They issued "no comment" edicts to the Cardinal and the press. But, no, not me! I had to give the Cardinal a basic civic lesson! Having been victimized by the abdication of state funding from the Casey and Ridge administrations over the past six years, the Upper Darby School District was financially strapped. I thought the Cardinal and his advisors had taken too much LSD! I wanted to tell the salivating reporters just that, but I behaved. I wrote a very "restrained" but tough letter to the Cardinal and shared it with the press:

> The Constitutional responsibility of all Pennsylvania School Boards, including Upper Darby, is to provide a "thorough and efficient" system of public education. As such, we have no desire to expend monies for students in schools other than our own.
>
> Your suggestion of voucher payments to Catholic School parents would only drain money away from Upper Darby's public schools which already have tremendous financial problems.
>
> Our school system has tight accountability to the Commonwealth of Pennsylvania, and is audited in many different areas. Should you accept public monies for Catholic schools, it is likely that your schools would be accountable to public authorities as I am. It is hard for me to believe that the Arch-

diocese of Philadelphia would welcome any oversight from the state. Even worse, you might have to accept some of the special needs children that my public schools already educate in abundance!

Further, we are aware of no ground swell of Catholic students who are already in my public schools wishing to transfer to Catholic schools. As a result, if we follow your plan, we would simply be taking money from our schools to subsidize yours. And why in the name of heaven would we want to do that?

As a Catholic, I was more than a little uncomfortable telling off the Cardinal. But then again, why should His Eminence merit special consideration? He asked. I answered. Big Deal! What was I supposed to do? He created the news media box. There was no other way out. Gee, I wonder if I've been excommunicated?

35

THE NAZI MENACE

In the early 1990s, Upper Darby High had a population of about twenty-five hundred students. Among that group were eight pupils who considered themselves to be skinheads. They were into shaved heads, tattoos, leather outfits, heavy black boots, and Nazi rhetoric.

I've always wondered what type of parents would allow this type of crap inside their homes. You see, I just have a very difficult time comprehending the impotence of any family's adults in cases like this. How could parents tolerate such ridiculous behavior from their children? Silly me!

One afternoon about a hour or so after school had been dismissed, this Nazi army and a few outsiders of similar persuasion were marching back and forth on the school campus like the silly clowns they were. They were on a war mission. Eventually, three targets exited the high school into their web. Achtung, Heil Hitler, and all that garbage! They ganged up on the victims and punched and kicked them in an assault that lasted for a few minutes. Then, three or four of my football players came to the rescue of the beaten, and the Nazi army retreated to their bunkers or wherever they came from.

The news media had a field day with this one. *Armed gangs of Nazis were terrorizing the school. Tension and turmoil at Upper Darby High School!* Give me a break!

Within a day or so, the high school administrators had captured all of the Nazis. It wasn't real hard! There were of course three witnesses, but these eight ridiculous perpetrators stood out as bright spotlights among the student body. You couldn't miss these bald-headed dunces in a crowd, and we didn't. We moved to expel them all. Terroristic threats. Ethnic intimidation. A host of school discipline code violations. Each skinhead soon had legal representation. This had little effect on me. By this time, I was quite used to lawyers threatening me. I had developed immunity to legal viruses. Someone from the ACLU called and expressed interest in joining the defense team. They had better hurry, I told them. These kids were dead meat.

I had never met a true leader of the Aryan League. Matter of fact, I didn't know there was any such organization anywhere near Upper Darby. But sure enough, everything happens to me. The guy lived in the community and as a taxpayer demanded the right to talk to me. He made an appointment and showed up late one afternoon.

He was not what I expected. This *commandant* did not have a shaved head, but he did have a blond ivy hair cut and piercing blue eyes. He was soft-spoken. And he was creepy! "We have decided that you are the one person who can help us, and you will do so!" he decreed. "Tomorrow, you will have all of the charges dropped against my young men. In return, we will be on our best behavior at the school and cause no further problems. It is a compromise that both sides can live with."

I politely told this loony that he was out of his mind. That all eight expulsion hearings would be held as scheduled in the next week. And that there would *not* be any deals made in this case.

"Ah, Mr. Superintendent, you have not understood all the conditions," this Nazi jerk continued. "We know *where you live*. If you free our soldiers, we will forget where you live. That is the part of an offer you can't possibly refuse."

I tried to keep cool. "Listen, you Nazi fool," I monotoned, "you have just stepped over the goddamned line. You have just threatened an officer of the Commonwealth of Pennsylvania. You have three seconds to exit this office. Otherwise, you're gonna have to deal with me here now, instead of the Upper Darby police."

The Nazi shrugged and threw up his hands symbolically. He smiled ominously like he wouldn't be responsible for what would happen now. He left quietly like he came. I gasped for air! When I stopped trembling, I called the cops. They would send someone over immediately to take a report on the incident.

During the next week, I was more than a little bit nervous. But the proceedings went off like clockwork. Eight Upper Darby High School students were exiled forever. And I was even still alive.

The day after the last expulsion hearing, a couple of Upper Darby detectives came to see me. They had followed up on my incident report on the personal threat from the Nazi commander. They had gone to his apartment to tell him to back off of me. However, there was no sign of the Nazi. It appeared that he had permanently left. His apartment was cleaned out. He had settled his account with his landlord and said he was moving to Florida.

36

I AM MY
FATHER'S SON

This book would not be complete without my telling you about my father. *Nobody* in my life influenced me more than he did. My values and personality come from him. To begin, I should tell you that he died in 1980 without ever knowing that his son would become a superintendent of schools. I'm sure the very idea would have blown him away!

Ben was a very private man. By America's materialistic standards, he wasn't too successful. He started as a maintenance man at the General Electric factory and ended up in the same position thirty-five years later. He was very conscientious and never missed a day of work.

In terms of worldly possessions, our family never had much. But I had some real riches in my dad. At night, he was usually dog tired and went to bed early. But every morning, he would rise at 5:00 A.M. and brew coffee, and cook whatever was in the house for breakfast. I would smell the coffee on schedule, wake up, and wander down to the kitchen to be alone with my dad.

And did we ever talk! During those early morning hours, he was no longer a shy maintenance man. For he had the ability each morning to mutate into some wonderful combination that was partially an eloquent professor, a sermonizing priest, a perceptive news analyst, and an all-wise Supreme Court justice.

These mornings were special times when a father and his son were very close. We would hold philosophic conversations about the rightness and wrongness of things, about decency, about honesty, about courage, about caring for people less fortunate, and about trying to improve the world in which we lived.

CHAPTER 36

Like some learned guru, my father illustrated values and principles with examples he picked out from current events, politics, sports, and things that happened at work or in the neighborhood.

So here we had the maintenance man in Southwest Philly who was turned into an all-knowing philosopher, clarifying, moralizing, and giving meaning to life like some great sage. He may not have been Aristotle, Socrates, Ghandi, or Confucius but he was doing their thing, imparting wisdom to the willing teenage pupil.

When my father died, he left behind no lucrative will to change the lives of his wife and five children. But he bequeathed to me a very valuable legacy. For how do you put a price on altruism, morality, and ethical conduct? Those were the life priorities he instilled in me, and I've tried to live by them. The most important things for humankind. *Words from the prophet, Ben, my father, the best teacher I ever had:*

1. You stand up for principle regardless of the consequences.
2. You do your homework; then you speak out for what is right.
3. Laugh at yourself, and people will laugh with you, not at you.
4. Integrity is like virginity; lose it, and it's gone forever.
5. Prioritize concern for the less fortunate; underdogs need a voice!
6. Power corrupts; your soul is not for sale to the rich and famous.
7. It's okay to be afraid; that's what true courage is all about.
8. Always give a damn about what is morally correct.

37

LOVE STORY

The best way for me to summarize my fifteen years as superintendent of schools in Upper Darby is to tell you that it was a love affair. Like any relationship, there were hills and valleys and ups and downs. But the overall experience was wonderful. And there was an overwhelming sense of fulfillment, because so much of what I did made some difference for the better. My heart is full of memorable joys. This could only be love!

The Upper Darby School District community represents the very best in hard-working, caring, and decent people. Living and laboring there was as fulfilling as it gets. I have had the exhilaration of seeing literally thousands of students achieve and accomplish with the knowledge that I had played some part in this. It just doesn't get any better.

In the Upper Darby School District, I was surrounded by teachers and administrators and support staff who truly cared about the education of the young people they served. I'd like to think I was at least partially responsible for the development of that ethic.

Over the years, I guest taught in various schools on more than one hundred occasions. I wanted to be part of the action, to be where things really mattered. Not only does this superintendent go out to teach, but he's damn good at it! Just ask any teacher whose class I've taught!

My favorite school district thing was chatting with kids about their schooling, and with anyone else who would listen about what we were trying to do to educate those kids. By the time I retired, I had personal relationships with hundreds and hundreds of students, colleagues, parents, and other community residents. I prowled most of the community's stores, and Joan and I were highly visible neighborhood walkers and talkers.

During my tenure, I was present at more than four hundred consecutive school board meetings. Even I'm in awe of that number! Move over, Lou Gehrig—I never missed a game either! If you'd like, I can take off my shirt and show you all my many war scars. I experienced forty-nine different school board members and eight board presidents. The vast majority of them exemplified standards of public service at the highest levels. Lots of them are still my good friends.

I estimate that I attended well in excess of fourteen hundred school events and activities while I was superintendent. My most terrifying experience was being the guest conductor of the senior high's vaunted Concert Band. I much preferred just being a fan at football games. And finally, I delivered about six hundred formal speeches inside and outside the community during that time. I attempted to stand up for what I believed regardless of the consequences. That's what superintendents of schools are supposed to be all about.

There are no adequate words to describe this love affair. It was a whirlwind ride of passion that touched my soul. I am honored and humbled to have had the experience.

EPILOGUE

The limousine was parked directly outside the Overbrook Italian Club, located in Philadelphia just a few miles from Upper Darby. Well-dressed bodyguards loitered about the exterior of the building on patrol.

Inside the members only club, Sal, Rocco, Guido, and Joey were having lunch. Sal was feasting on two pounds of calamari swimming in red gravy; he was addicted to the stuff. Rocco was forking down a small antipasto; he had to preserve his well-honed body. Guido was devouring a huge plate of garbanzo beans; he loved the suckers. And Joey was slurping down a humongous garlicky bowl of spaghetti in oil with anchovies, his favorite food in the world. Fresh baked Italian bread, roasted hot peppers, and bottles of Chianti filled their table to overflowing.

Sal stopped eating for a moment and proposed a toast. "Here's to you, Joey. Just like Frank, you did it your way! And what a helluva party that was last night!"

The quartet clanged their glasses and drank down their fifth glass of Chianti. Sal's reference had been to Joey's "sold out" retirement banquet at Philadelphia's Twelve Caesar's Restaurant the previous night. The Upper Darby School District community had turned out in force to formally say a gala goodbye to its long-term superintendent of schools. This afternoon, the four men were finishing the retirement celebration.

"Sal, I don't want to spoil this feast we're having, but I'd like to ask you just one question," Joey inquired. "I've been wondering for a long time about that Nazi leader who left town in such a hurry. Were you guys involved in his departure?"

Sal and Rocco winked at each other knowingly. Then Sal responded: "Joey, if we tell you this, I want a promise upfront that you'll do somethin' for us." This sounded ominous, but Joey rapidly agreed. He wanted to know.

"We knew that this Nazi had come to see you, and that he was probably planning to cause you some trouble. So Rocco and Guido had a serious talk with him! We didn't offer him any choices. He was very willing to leave town when we asked him. We might have had to do something more drastic, but it wasn't necessary. End of story.

"Now, Joey, here's our request. We've heard that you're gonna write a book. First you become a superintendent of schools! Now, you're gonna be an author. So here's the deal. Rocco, Guido, and me want to be in the book. Promise us you'll write us into the goddamned thing. The three of us wants to be immortals."

"Consider it done," Joey told Sal, using one of Sal's well-used phrases. "There's no way I could ever write my book without the three of you being in there with me. Let's drink to it." The foursome drank down round six of Chianti. Life was good!

Here are the most important messages I learned as a school superintendent and elsewhere:

- Great teachers make the difference for *all* students, and especially the kids everyone else has written off.
- Good school administrators *do what they have to do* in this world.
- If you need something to happen and it's not happening, *act like a maniac*.
- *You can't deny your roots* or run from your past.
- Comparing schools or school districts via standardized tests results just validates socioeconomic inequality.
- A good superintendent often has to be *tough and solitary especially when principle is involved.*
- Good school superintendents *stand up* when they have to. You don't back off from bullies trying to destroy public schools.

- Public education has always been and continues to be a remarkably effective institution for those who opt to take advantage of the marvelous opportunities it provides.
- Fairness is definitely not a concept with which the news media is familiar.
- The public's right to know really means *the public's right to know what editors and reporters decide to tell them.*
- School administrators need to fight back much more than they're doing at present. *It's about doing what's right.* And there's no room for cowardice here.
- *As a leader, you define, demand, inspire, motivate, reinforce, and compliment.* And then, you get the hell out of the way.
- Parents make the difference for their children more than any other factor.
- Being a superintendent of schools is first and foremost about being on the *moral high ground.*

BIBLIOGRAPHY

Berliner, David C., and Bruce J. Biddle. *The Manufactured Crisis*. Reading, MA: Addison-Wesley, 1995.

Berliner, David C., and Bruce J. Biddle. "The Lamentable Alliance Between the Media and School Critics," *The School Administrator* September 1998 (12–18).

Bracey, Gerard W. *Setting the Record Straight*. Alexandria, VA: Association for Supervision and Curriculum Development, 1997.

Carson, C.C., R.M. Huelskamp, and T.D. Woodall. "Perspectives on Education in America," *Journal of Educational Research* May/June 1993 (261–310).

Kozol, Jonathan. *Savage Inequalities: Children in America's Schools*. New York: Crown, 1991.

Rubin, Lillian Breslow. *Worlds of Pain*. New York: Basic Books, 1976.

Troy, Forrest J. "The Myth of Our Failed Education System," *The School Administrator* September 1998 (6–10).

ABOUT THE AUTHOR

Joe Batory was the Upper Darby (PA) School District's Superintendent of Schools from 1984 to 1999 when he retired. He has been recognized for his numerous accomplishments as a public school leader with the Distinguished Lifetime Service Award from the American Association of School Administrators (2000). Additionally, in 1990, he was named as one of The Executive Educator 100, a group of only 100 outstanding school leaders chosen from America's 300,000 school administrators by a distinguished panel of independent jurors, all expert in the field.

Batory was cited with the Pennsylvania Music Educators' 1997 Superintendent of the Year award for his outstanding support of music programs in public schools. He has also received the 1998 Friend of Journalism award from the Pennsylvania School Press Association.

His service to children has been recognized with other awards from the Rotary Club of Upper Darby (1999 and 1989), the Delaware County Chamber of Commerce (1999), the Study Councils of the University of Pennsylvania (1999), the Delaware County Intermediate Unit (1999), the Patriotic Order of Sons of America (1992), the Upper Darby Teachers' Association (1999), Transport Workers Union Local 289 (1999), the Upper Darby Administrators and Supervisors Association (1999), the Upper Darby Educational Support Personnel (1999), the Drexel Hill Baptist Church (1999), and the National School Public Relations Association (1989).